And More Celebrating the Seasons with Children

Feb 1987

D1374242

And More Celebrating the Seasons with Children

*Conversation Ideas
Based on the Common Lectionary
Year A*

PHILIP E. JOHNSON

THE PILGRIM PRESS
New York

The biblical quotations in this book are from the
Revised Standard Version of the Bible, copyright 1946,
1952, and © 1971, 1973 by the Division of Christian
Education, National Council of Churches, and are used
with permission. In some cases the quotations have been
adapted by the author.

Library of Congress Cataloging-in-Publication Data

Johnson, Philip E., 1943–
  And more celebrating the seasons with children.

  Includes indexes.
  1. Children's sermons—Outlines, syllabi, etc.
  2. Bible—Homiletical use. I. Title.
  BV4315.J62 1986   251'.02   86-12387
  ISBN 0-8298-0735-7 (pbk.)

The Pilgrim Press, 132 West 31 Street, New York, NY 10001

To
Jill Elizabeth
and
Timothy Gordon

CONTENTS

ACKNOWLEDGMENTS

Special thanks to:

All children with whom I have shared precious moments, especially in worship.

The ministers of Maple Grove United Church, Oakville, Ontario, Canada, whose pastor I am and whose journey of faith I am privileged to share.

Joy Lawrence, my friend in Christ, who has prepared my manuscript with love and excellence.

David Peacock, my friend, whose creative spirit inspires and delights through art.

Lyn, my wife, who by her love, patience, encouragement, and gracious presence makes every day a celebration.

INTRODUCTION

And More Celebrating the Seasons with Children provides pastors, church school teachers, and other group leaders with a collection of tested, stimulative ideas for inclusive conversations with children aged four to eight years, in the context of Christian worship or other Christian educational settings.

The ideas emerge from the biblical readings for Year A of the *Common Lectionary* and therefore follow the flow and emphasis of the seasons of the liturgical year. With the exception of the season of Pentecost, for which the readings do not have a thematic unity, I have developed a theme common to the readings for the day and have suggested a title, resources, and a prayer. These conversations can also be used by those who are following *An Inclusive Language Lectionary,* Year A, and, of course, by those who follow no lectionary.

Persons telling the Christian story are affirmed and encouraged to integrate their own faith, imagination, and creativity in their own particular situation. Children are also affirmed and encouraged to appropriate a sense of the story of God's interaction with humankind as their own story. In addition, they are invited to experience the richness of God's grace now through the faithful personhood of and interaction with the storyteller.

Planning well in advance is important. I have found it advantageous to plan about a year ahead in order to coordinate my conversations with the lectionary readings and with events in the life of the congregation, such as anniversary Sunday or the annual stewardship campaign. This resource will assist you as a catalyst in the planning process. My suggestions are not to be followed slavishly, but are to be a springboard for your own faithful creativity. For example, if the object referred to is not available, a picture of the object or a substitute object can be used. Always choose objects that help to communicate your message.

Care must be exercised if you are having a conversation with *children* in the context of worship. A children's hymn during which they gather at the front can effectively draw them together without "putting them on display" and can indicate to them that they indeed have a special place in the Christian community. I sit down with the children at the front and wear a microphone because I discovered a long time ago that adults are influenced profoundly by what is said to the children. Take care also to ensure that whatever is said or done is appropriate to worship and that each child is attended to in the spirit of Christ. The greatest gift a storyteller can give is the gift of his or her presence.

To celebrate means to keep or to remember. This book is intended truly to celebrate the seasons of the church year with children!

The Season of Advent

"Anticipation Bulbs"

Lesson 1: Isaiah 2:2–5
Lesson 2: Romans 13:11–14
Gospel: Matthew 24:36–44

Theme: Anticipating the birth of Christ

Resources: Firm, paper white narcissus bulbs—five or six for the church container and one for each child—treated for forcing (store the bulbs in a cool place until ready to plant); a container filled with small stones; water

Development: Advent marks the beginning of the Christian year. Its seasonal color, purple, suggests an essential reflective nature to this four-week period of preparation for celebrating Jesus' birth. Advent looks forward, just as people centuries ago longed for the birth of the Messiah who would restore Israel.

Today's readings illustrate well the advent themes of prophecy and fulfillment, expectation and hope, admonition and warning. Isaiah prophesies a time when people throughout the world will worship God and live with one another in peace: "They shall beat their swords into plowshares, and their spears into pruning hooks; nation shall not lift up sword against nation, neither shall they learn war any more [Isa. 2:4]." Paul, in the second lesson, summarizes the heart of the law and urges the Romans to keep awake, for their salvation is near. The Gospel writer exhorts: "Watch therefore, for you do not know on what day your Sovereign is coming [Matt. 24:42]."

A common theme in these readings is anticipation, which can be beautifully communicated by the use of paper white narcissus bulbs. Plant these "anticipation bulbs" with the children today and around Christmas (be careful not to commit yourself to a specific date for blooming!) you'll have lots of starlike white (the liturgical color of Christmas) blossoms. Nestle five or six bulbs fat side down in a container filled with small stones, and add water until the bulbs are partially covered. Place the container in a cool but light location, and turn it and add water occasionally. Give each child an "anticipation bulb" to take home and plant. The obvious growth of the bulb throughout Advent at home and at church will graphically enable the children genuinely to anticipate the birth of Christ.

Prayer: Creator of all, we are anticipating Jesus' birthday! Amen.

ADVENT 2

Run Up the Flag!

Lesson 1: Isaiah 11:1–10
Lesson 2: Romans 15:4–13
Gospel: Matthew 3:1–12

Theme: The coming of the Messiah
Resources: Flag (preferably the Christian flag); a flagpole

Development: The "anticipation bulbs" planted last week will already be sprouting, confirming the hopeful nature of the advent season. Be sure to engage the children in the growth process over the next few weeks. Expectations run high at this time of year anyway and escalate toward Christmas Day, especially for children. So go with the flow this Sunday! Heighten the religious anticipation by focusing on the One who is to come and what great things will take place on the

One's arrival. Paul, in the Epistle lesson, sets the stage for today's conversation by stating that when we know the story of how God's promises were fulfilled in the past, we may be filled with confidence and hope.

This Sunday probe the meaning of "our advent story" as recorded in the Gospel and the Old Testament lessons. Matthew pictures John the Baptist preaching in the wilderness of Judea, announcing the coming of the Messiah and urging the people to prepare for the Sovereign's judgment. This aspect of judgment is found also in Isaiah's news about God's appointed deliverer: "There shall come forth a shoot from the stump of Jesse, and a branch shall grow out of its roots. And the Spirit of God shall rest upon this branch, the spirit of wisdom and understanding, the spirit of counsel and might, the spirit of knowledge and the fear of God [Isa. 11:1–2]." This promised "branch" ushers in not only a time of judgment, but also a time of peace and cooperation, which Isaiah describes with vivid imagery. The promised One will stand out as a visible sign of hope: "In that day the root of Jesse shall stand as an ensign to the peoples that this is the One whom the nations shall seek, whose dwellings shall be glorious [Isa. 11:10]."

Run up a flag on a flagpole to demonstrate how all people, including us, will know of and "see" God's promise and be filled with hope as we approach Christmas.

Prayer: God of all people everywhere, we thank you for keeping your promise and sending the Messiah. Amen.

ADVENT 3

"I Can Hear!"

Lesson 1: Isaiah 35:1–10
Lesson 2: James 5:7–10
Gospel: Matthew 11:2–11

Theme: God saves the people
Resource: Soundproof earmuffs, or cotton batting

Development: Isaiah, in the first reading, envisions a time of abundance and healing for Israel, a time when "the wilderness and the dry land shall be glad, the desert shall rejoice and blossom; like the crocus it shall blossom abundantly, and rejoice with joy and singing [Isa. 35:1–2]." If you planted "anticipation bulbs" on the first Sunday of Advent, you may want to tie in the image of the crocus.

God will lead the people to fullness of life by divine transforming power, and the "new exodus" will begin. "Then the eyes of the blind shall be opened, and the ears of the deaf unstopped; then shall the lame leap like a hart, and the tongues of the dumb sing for joy [Isa. 35:5–6]." A similar image is expressed by Jesus in the Gospel, when he responds to a question from John the Baptist about his mission and describes John's ministry: "The blind receive their sight and the lame walk, lepers are cleansed and the deaf hear [Matt. 11:5]."

Enable the children to sense the excitement inherent in these readings for the great things that will take place by the gracious fulfillment of God's promise. Soon they will experience the wonders of Christmas for themselves. Although children may not understand Messiahship, they will be able to grasp the wonder of God's action in causing the deaf to hear! A pair of soundproof earmuffs can help you make the point. Just as those who are deaf rejoice when they hear for themselves, we celebrate our salvation in the birth of Christ when we experience Christmas. You may wish to use one of the other images, such as the blind seeing, to reinforce the theme.

Prayer: Dear God, who helps the deaf to hear, help us really to celebrate Christmas. Amen.

ADVENT 4

Jesus Emmanuel Carpenter

Lesson 1: Isaiah 7:10–16
Lesson 2: Romans 1:1–7
Gospel: Matthew 1:18–25

Theme: The Holy Child is named
Resources: A birth certificate; an "enlarged" birth certificate for Jesus, on bristol board

Development: People's names and their meanings have always fascinated me. To some degree, our personal names define us. The readings today, on the Sunday before Christmas Day, give us insight into the names given to the Holy Child at birth.

Show the children your birth certificate, and point out the date and place of birth and your names and their meanings. For example, my first name, Philip, comes from two Greek words: *philos*, which means "lover," and *hippos*, which means "horse." So my name literally means "lover of horses." Before your conversation with the children today, find out the meaning of two or three of their names, and then share those meanings with them.

Hold up an "enlarged" birth certificate for the Holy Child with the pertinent information: December 25, Bethlehem of Judea. Convey the meaning of the names Jesus Emmanuel Carpenter. In the Old Testament, the prophet Isaiah says that "a young woman shall conceive and bear a child whom she shall call Emmanuel [Isa. 7:14]." Emmanuel means "God with us." In the Gospel, an angel of God appears to Joseph in a dream and tells him that Mary will "bear a child, whose name you shall call Jesus, for this child will save the people from their sins [Matt. 1:21]." "Carpenter" is a somewhat fictitious surname to reflect Jesus' family connection. In closing, indicate that we are all special children in God's family and that God knows us by name.

Prayer: O God, thank you for Jesus Emmanuel Carpenter, our Savior. Amen.

The Christmas Season

Name and Address Please

Lesson 1: Isaiah 9:2–7
Lesson 2: Titus 2:11–14
Gospel: Luke 2:1–20

Theme: The birth of Christ
Resources: Buttons on which "Christmas Census" is printed

Development: The readings for today continue the theme of "name" considered in Advent 4 and provide an interesting possibility for your conversation with the children on this festival occasion. The glorious story of the birth of Christ must certainly be the focus, and my suggestions here serve to underline the "good news of a great joy which will come to all the people [Luke 2:10]."

The Old Testament passage, a hymn of thanks and hope, records how "the people who walked in darkness have seen a great light; those who dwelt in a land of deep darkness, on them has light shined [Isa. 9:2]." The light is the Holy Child whose "name will be called 'Wonderful Counselor, Mighty God, Everlasting Father and Mother, Ruler of Peace [Isa. 9:6].' " The Gospel picks up on the theme of name as the chapter begins, by setting the context for the birth of Jesus: "In those days a decree went out from Caesar Augustus that all the world should be enrolled. . . . And all went to be enrolled. . . . And Joseph also went up from Galilee, from the city of Nazareth, to Judea, to the city of David, which is called Bethlehem, because he was of the house and lineage of David, to be enrolled with Mary, his betrothed, who was with child [Luke 2:1, 3–5]." Jesus was born during a census, a gathering of names!

Conduct a census in which everyone can be "enrolled," and thereby personally identify with the action in the Christmas story. If you are having a conversation in the context of worship, the census would best be done at a table as people gather. You might have the names and addresses entered in an official-looking book and then place it in the church library or archives as a record of your census. Give every person who registers a button on which "Christmas Census" is printed. Simply read the Christmas story during your conversation. The children will truly experience Christmas with Mary and Joseph in Bethlehem!

Prayer: Happy birthday, Baby Jesus! Amen.

CHRISTMAS 1

The Great Escape

Lesson 1:   Isaiah 63:7–9
Lesson 2:   Hebrews 2:10–18
Gospel: Matthew 2:13–15, 19–23

Theme: God is with us
Resources: An infant carrier; a baby

Development: Some Christian communities have designated the first Sunday of this three-part season Holy Family Sunday. It is an opportunity to recognize not only the intriguing events in the lives of Mary, Joseph, and the baby Jesus, but also the essential role God plays in our family life. Keep in mind that the children will be in a reentry mood after their Christmas orbit and will still be on vacation.

The first two readings support the Gospel, which tells the fast-moving dramatic story of how the Holy

Family, by God's grace, made "the great escape" from Bethlehem to Egypt and traveled, subsequently, to their home, Nazareth. Set the stage for the conversation by painting a verbal picture of the principal characters in Bethlehem, just to remind the children of the context. Your Christmas Eve/Day reading of the Christmas story will have prepared them well. Help them figuratively to be with you and the Holy Family in the stable and then to experience, as fully as possible, the escape. In order to involve the children in this way, you must thoroughly prepare your mind and spirit with a solid knowledge and flow of the passage so that together you all can run for your lives!

Use an infant carrier to demonstrate how Jesus was still an infant when these events occurred. Of course, a live baby in the carrier will add a realistic dimension to your story-telling. Point out that just as God was with Mary and Joseph and Jesus long ago on their journey, so God is with our families today on our journey.

Prayer: Dear Mother and Father God, thank you for being with the Holy Family and with my family. Amen.

CHRISTMAS 2

God Becomes Flesh

Lesson 1: Jeremiah 31:7–14
Lesson 2: Ephesians 1:3–6, 15–18
Gospel: John 1:1–18

Theme: God became a human being
Resources: An infant; a Christ Candle

Development: The startling, surprising joyous reality of Christmas is that God became a human being! The Gospel according to John begins with a classic theological statement of the mystery of the incarnation: "In the beginning was the Word, and the Word was with God, and the Word was God. . . . In the Word was life, and the life was the light of all. . . . The true light that enlightens everyone was coming into the world. . . . And the Word became flesh and dwelt among us [John 1:1, 4, 9, 14]." The Word became flesh! What an exciting message we have to convey to the children that God loved us enough to be revealed in the form of a baby!

The first and second readings today are certainly supportive of the Gospel lesson and focus solely on the theme indicated: the Old Testament reading records how God saved the people of Israel and brought them home to Zion; the letter to the Ephesians praises God's glorious grace in Jesus Christ.

Invite the children to gather in a circle around the Christ Candle. Hold an infant in your arms, and from your own faithful center, tell the story of the incarnation so that the children can sense the mystery of God's love unfolding before them. Light the Christ Candle to communicate that the birth of God's Holy Child was like light shining in the darkness. Allow the beauty and the powerful nature of this image of the true light to penetrate your hearts and minds by spending a few quiet moments together before the prayer.

Prayer: True Light of the World, we praise you. Come shine in our hearts today. Amen.

Epiphany and the Season Following

"Starlight"

Lesson 1: Isaiah 60:1–6
Lesson 2: Ephesians 3:1–12
Gospel: Matthew 2:1–12

Theme: Jesus Christ, the true light, is born
Resources: A map of the stars; a telescope

Development: Epiphany, from a Greek word meaning manifestation or appearance, is the season that reveals God's love in Christ, the true light. It not only heralds the birth of the light, but also traces the spreading of the light to all people. Some faith communities will celebrate this liturgical day with a joyous festival of lights—a kind of second Christmas.

On Christmas 2, we prepared the children to make a smooth transition to the season of Epiphany. Having literally gathered around the burning Christ Candle, they will have already "seen the light." Today that theme of light continues as we consider Matthew's account of the "star" guiding the astrologers from the East to Bethlehem to worship the One born ruler of the Jews.

The Old Testament and the Gospel are closely connected. Isaiah announces the return of the exiles to Jerusalem—"Arise, shine; for your light has come, and the glory of God has risen upon you [Isa. 60:1]"—and then predicts the eschatological pilgrimage of the gentiles to Jerusalem that will follow the rebuilding of the city. These two ideas from the prophet are paralleled in the Gospel by the incarnation and the journey of the magi.

Explore the wonder and mystery inherent in the Gospel by using a map of the stars, a telescope, or other resources, such as posters or slides. Good friends of mine registered a star in my name for my birthday so my use of the accompanying map and certificate added a personal touch. Just as you enabled the children to escape from Bethlehem with the Holy Family, help them today to travel to the birthplace of Christ with the astrologers. It's an exciting journey with a joyous conclusion!

Prayer: Creator of the stars, we praise you! Shine on me today. Amen.

EPIPHANY 1
(BAPTISM OF OUR SOVEREIGN)

Light Before Your Eyes

Lesson 1: Isaiah 42:1–9
Lesson 2: Acts 10:34–43
Gospel: Matthew 3:13–17

Theme: Jesus' baptism: a light to the nations
Resource: A globe of the world that can be lighted from inside

Development: Epiphany originated in the East, where it was primarily a commemoration of Jesus' baptism. On the first epiphany, Jesus was baptized by John as a sign of Jesus' servanthood; it was similar to the ancient usage of the word epiphany to describe a ruler "showing" himself or having an audience before the people of the nation. Focus today on Jesus' baptism and how the light of God's presence in Christ is a light not only to individuals referred to in Christmas 2 and Epiphany, but to all the people of the world as well.

Isaiah the prophet, in the first "servant song,"

speaks of the mission of God's servant whom God has chosen to bring justice and salvation: "I have called you in righteousness, I have taken you by the hand and kept you; I have given you as a covenant to the people, a light to the nations, to open the eyes that are blind, to bring out the prisoners from the dungeon, from the prison those who sit in gloom [Isa. 42:6–7]." Communicate to the children that Jesus' baptism calls us all to be servants of God and, like Jesus, to be a blessed light to the nations. A globe that can be lighted from inside demonstrates well how the light of God in Christ shines in our world. You may want to use a flat map glued to a solid backing through which Christmas lights can be placed on the continents. However you do it, assist the children to understand that through their baptism, they share with Christ the mission of being light to the world.

Prayer: O God, Light to all the nations, shine on all people everywhere. Amen.

EPIPHANY 2

Ba-a-a-a! Ba-a-a-a!

Lesson 1: Isaiah 49:1–7
Lesson 2: 1 Corinthians 1:1–9
Gospel: John 1:29–41   3-88

Theme: Jesus, the Lamb of God
Resource: A lamb

Development: The Old Testament lesson is Isaiah's second "servant song," which describes poetically the one who will bring people to an awareness of God's power, justice, and love. The servant will suffer so that the people can be restored to God after their separation. Isaiah reflects on the servant's mission and sees God's high calling and how God promises to be with the servant even in times of difficulty. Similarly, the mission of Jesus is the central theme of the Gospel: "[John the Baptist] saw Jesus coming toward him, and said, 'Behold, the Lamb of God, who takes away the sin of the world [John 1:29]!' "

The "lamb of God" was an important symbol to the Jews. In Exodus, chapter 12, we read the instructions that at the Passover, an unblemished lamb be slaughtered and consumed by the people. This was understood as a means of reconciling the people to God through the sacrifice of what was called the Paschal, or Passover, Lamb. The disciples came to appreciate that Jesus was the true Paschal Lamb that takes away the sins of the world.

Bring our rich ritual heritage alive today by having a live lamb present. The children will not forget the day we had the lamb in church! Give them some insight at their level about the Passover practices, and share how Jesus is recognized as the forgiving lamb for all time. Conclude by assuring them that Jesus' sacrifice on the cross long ago is a sign that God has forgiven our sin too.

Prayer: O Lamb of God, who takes away the sin of the world, thank you for forgiving my sin. Amen.

Ekklesia

Lesson 1: Isaiah 9:1–4
Lesson 2: 1 Corinthians 1:10–17
Gospel: Matthew 4:12–23

Theme: The ministry of the "called-out" people
Resources: EKKLESIA printed in extra large letters on a piece of bristol board or newsprint; a pocket radio; an invitation card; an adhesive bandage

Development: "The people who walked in gloom have seen a great light; those who dwelt in a land of deep shadows, on them has light shined [Isa. 9:2]." With these words of promise from God to Israel, the prophet's role is established. He is called by God to bring justice and mercy. The Gospel picks up on the Old Testament reference to calling by quoting the same passage from Isaiah and then describing how Jesus called the fishers. " 'Follow me,' " Jesus said to Peter and Andrew as they walked by the Sea of Galilee, " 'and I will make you fishers of women and men.' Immediately they left their nets and followed him [Matt. 4:19–20]."

Explain today, using a piece of bristol board on which is printed in large letters EKKLESIA, that our word church is derived from the Greek *ekklēsia*, which literally means "called out (*ek* is the Greek word for 'out' and *klesia* comes from *kaleo*, 'to call')." Relate that just as Jesus called out the fishers, we, too, are called out to be God's people, the church.

Jesus' ministry was threefold: he proclaimed the coming of the realm, called the disciples, and performed miracles of healing. Similarly, our threefold ministry as those who are called out is to preach the gospel, call people to discipleship, and heal the sick.

Communicate the three aspects of our ministry by using a pocket radio, an invitation card, and an adhesive bandage. Once you have explained the meaning of *ekklēsia*, ask the children what these three objects have in common; then explain our challenging ministry in the name of Christ.

Prayer: Thank you for calling me out to be an important part of your body, the church. Amen.

EPIPHANY 4

Order! Order!

Lesson 1: Micah 6:1–8
Lesson 2: 1 Corinthians 1:18–31
Gospel: Matthew 5:1–12

Theme: What God requires
Resources: A judge's gown; a gavel

Development: There are many conversation possibilities presented by the readings today. The Epistle lesson is Paul's letter to the church at Corinth about the wisdom of God and how worldly standards of wisdom and foolishness are to be put aside. The Gospel is a portion of Jesus' Sermon on the Mount, in which the "model" teacher offers words of comfort and challenge about blessedness or true happiness. In the Old Testament lesson, Micah describes a controversy between the God of Israel and the people.

This passage from Micah is a splendid opportunity to pull out all the dramatic stops. God and Israel are having an argument! Children can relate to that. But this is an argument on a grand scale. Wear a judge's gown, and begin the conversation by sounding the gavel and calling "Order! Order!" Set the scene so they know who is arguing. The case is pleaded before the mountains, who are the jury. Point out that God speaks out against the people, reminding them of all the divine saving acts with which they have been blessed. Exaggerate, to give the feeling of a larger-than-life court case: "O my people, what have I done to you? In what have I wearied you? Answer me [Mic. 6:3]!" The passage need not be memorized and cue cards are permitted. The key is that your spirit is in harmony with the story. Israel asks what it should offer to God, and God answers with clarity and gentleness: "God has showed you, O people, what is good; and what does the Sovereign One require of you but to do justice, and to love kindness, and to walk humbly with your God [Mic. 6:8]?"

Close today's conversation after the prayer with the phrase "Court is adjourned."

Prayer: Dear God, I will do justice, love kindness, and walk humbly with you. Amen.

EPIPHANY 5

You Are the Light of the World!

Lesson 1: Isaiah 58:5–10
Lesson 2: 1 Corinthians 2:1–5
Gospel: Matthew 5:13–16

Theme: You are the light of the world
Resources: An oil lamp; matches; a bushel basket; a folding ladder

Development: The season of Epiphany continues today with its emphasis on light. Isaiah provides an excellent background for a conversation based on the Gospel. The prophet indicates that what God requires in worship is not fasting, but justice: "Is it not to share your bread with the hungry, and bring the homeless poor into your house; when you see the naked, to cover them, and not to hide yourself from your own flesh [Isa. 58:7]?" The result of acting justly is summarized in the next verse: "Then shall your light break forth like the dawn [Isa. 58:8]."

Jesus, in the Gospel, also addresses the theme of light and says that the righteous are "the light of the world." What a powerful image! "You are the light of the world. A city set on a hill cannot be hid. No one lights a lamp and puts it under a bushel, but on a stand, and it gives light to all in the house [Matt. 5:14–15]." Light an oil lamp, and place a bushel that's fairly airtight over it to communicate that our light must never be prevented from burning brightly. The musical *Godspell* catches the intent of "You are the light of the world": "But if that light's under a bushel, it's lost something kind of crucial."

Express how our light must give light to all by relighting the lamp and carefully placing it on top of a folding ladder so that all can clearly see it. Encourage the children to shine brightly this week to glorify God. Close by giving Jesus' invitation and challenge: "Let your light so shine before others, that they may see your good works and give glory to God [Matt. 5:16]."

Prayer: True Light of the World, I'm shining brightly for you! Amen.

First . . . Then . . .

Lesson 1: Deuteronomy 30:15–20
Lesson 2: 1 Corinthians 2:6–13
Gospel: Matthew 5:17–26

Theme: Reconciliation with one's neighbor
Resource: An offering envelope with contents

Development: Two significant possibilities for conversations with the children emerge from the readings today. The Old Testament lesson treats the theme of the ultimate choice between life and death. The writer says: "I call heaven and earth to witness against you this day, that I have set before you life and death, blessing and curse; therefore choose life, that you and your descendants may live [Deut. 30:19]." It would be most beneficial to help children deal with the choices they have to make at their stage of life.

The other possibility, and the one I would select today, comes from the Gospel, in which Jesus contrasts the righteousness of those living in God's realm with the moralism of the Pharisees. "You have heard that it was said in ancient times, 'You shall not kill; and whoever kills shall be liable to judgment.' But I say to you that every one who is angry with a neighbor shall be liable to judgment [Matt. 5:21–22].'" The old law is not to be abandoned, but reinterpreted. Convey to the children that as God's people, our behavior must reflect the spirit of the law. Act out the story Jesus gave as an example of getting along with our neighbor: "So if you are offering your gift at the altar, and there remember that your neighbor has something against you, leave your gift there before the altar and go; first be reconciled to your neighbor, and then come and offer your gift [Matt. 5:23–24]."

Invite someone to play the role of the neighbor and to work with you toward reconciliation before you return to offer your gift at the altar. Your animation of the Gospel will enable the children truly to understand the story.

Prayer: God of law and love, teach me your way. Amen.

EPIPHANY 7

Building on the Block

Lesson 1: Isaiah 49:8–13
Lesson 2: 1 Corinthians 3:10–11, 16–23
Gospel: Matthew 5:27–37

Theme: Christ is the foundation of life
Resource: A cement block

Development: The Epistle lessons for Epiphany this year have not been directly connected to the thrust I have taken with the conversations with the children. Today, however, I would zero in on the strong image offered in Paul's letter to the church at Corinth. The other two appointed lessons do not need to be particularly explored in this regard. The Old Testament lesson is God's statement to the people of Israel about the restoration of Jerusalem and the invitation to "sing for joy, O heavens, and exult, O earth; break forth, O mountains, into singing! For the Sovereign One has comforted the people, and will have compassion on the afflicted [Isa. 49:13]." The Gospel is Jesus' teaching about adultery, divorce, and swearing, which may present difficulty in some settings.

The apostle Paul reminds the Corinthians that they are God's temple and that God's eternal spirit dwells in them. He sets out an understanding of the foundation of the Christian life and the resulting behavior that is expected. "According to the grace of God given to me, like a skilled builder I laid a foundation, and another one is building upon it. Let each person take care how it is built upon. For no other foundation can any one lay than that which is laid, which is Jesus Christ [1 Cor. 3:10–11]." Get across the idea of Jesus Christ being the one and only foundation of the Christian life by placing a cement block in full view of all the children. The size and weight of the block will signify the solid nature of this absolutely essential base.

Invite one of the children to stand on the block and then explain that every person that builds her or his life on this foundation of Christ is like a spiritual building, God's temple, in which the spirit of God lives. Affirm that all God's children are special people and encourage them consciously to build their lives on Christ this week.

Prayer: Spirit of God living in me, thanks for helping me to build my life each day on Christ. Amen.

EPIPHANY 8

Love the Bully?

Lesson 1: Leviticus 19:1–2, 9–18
Lesson 2: 1 Corinthians 4:1–5
Gospel: Matthew 5:38–48

Theme: Love your enemies
Resource: An eye patch, or eye makeup

Development: Both the Old Testament lesson and the Gospel lesson deal with the behavior expected of

God's people. In Leviticus, the people of Israel are called to lives of justice and love and to be holy in their relations with others because God is holy and to be revered. The response to God and one's neighbor must not be separated. "You shall not hate your neighbor in your heart, but you shall reason with your neighbor. . . . You shall not take vengeance or bear any grudge against any of your own people, but you shall love your neighbor as yourself [Lev. 19:17–18]."

The Gospel continues this theme in which Jesus tells the disciples to be merciful because God is merciful. Teaching about revenge, Jesus warns: "You have heard that it was said, 'An eye for an eye and a tooth for a tooth.' But I say to you, Do not resist one who is evil. But if any one strikes you on the right cheek, turn the other also [Matt. 5:38–39].'" A few verses later, Christ issues a startling statement of contrast: "You have heard that it was said, 'You shall love your neighbor and hate your enemy.' But I say to you, Love your enemies and pray for those who persecute you [Matt. 5:43–44]."

Focus primarily today on these two teachings of Jesus. To set the scene before your conversation, wear a patch over one eye or apply eye makeup to give the appearance that you have a "black eye." As the children gather, talk about Jesus' teaching about revenge, indicating as well that children occasionally must appropriately stand up for themselves, not to get even, but to protect their welfare. Then state Jesus' second teaching, and illustrate it by asking whether they know a "bully." Explain that Jesus wants them to love even the bully who causes a "black eye." Remove the patch and tell them that you wore it only to help them remember the story. Assure them that you are all right.

Love the bully? Yes indeed! In a world of increasing

aggression, children need to hear the gracious gospel of love.

Prayer: Loving God, help me to love even the bully. Amen.

EPIPHANY 9

Blinded by the Light

Lesson 1: Exodus 24:12–18
Lesson 2: 2 Peter 1:16–21
Gospel: Matthew 17:1–9

Theme: The transfiguration of Jesus
Resource: Flashlight

Development: The Gospel on this final Sunday of Epiphany relates how Jesus was transfigured in the presence of Peter, James, and John. This focus may be enhanced by the Old Testament's record of Moses coming to God on the mountain to receive the ten commandments. The sense of mystery that prevails in both these passages is what must be communicated today. In fact, the Epistle lesson speaks of true prophecy that comes through the inspiration of the Holy Spirit, and you may want to refer at some point to this aspect of God's activity.

The transfiguration experience is not only difficult to understand, but also to communicate. Tell how Jesus and his disciples went up on a high mountain away from everything and everyone. Enable the children to perceive this location as a unique place where wonderful things might happen by God's grace. Literally and gently unfold the story about how Jesus was transfigured before the disciples, the appearance of Moses and Elijah, the bright cloud covering them and the voice speaking, and the response of the disciples and Jesus. The passage uses symbolism and themes from Israel's rich past and its anticipated future. Indeed, Jesus fulfilled the ancient tradition represented by Moses and the law and Elijah and the prophets. A flashlight may be used effectively to help the children to grasp the mysterious nature of events. Carefully shine the flashlight into your eyes and express that all you can see is light. You may want to shine the flashlight in a couple of the children's eyes to get their response too. In the same way, then, when the disciples saw Jesus being transfigured before their eyes, they were "blinded by the light" of Christ, the true light of the world.

Prayer: God of Light, shine in my eyes and heart today. Amen.

The Season of Lent

From Ashes to Easter

Lesson 1: Joel 2:12–19
Lesson 2: 2 Corinthians 5:20b—6:10
Gospel: Matthew 6:1–6, 16–21

Theme: The spiritual journey from Ash Wednesday to Easter Sunday

Resources: A pair of binoculars; a round, liturgically colored target

Development: Ash Wednesday begins the season of Lent, which is a time to reflect on God's action in history and the covenants made between God and the people. In the early Christian church, Lent was a period of intense preparation for those seeking baptism, and the emphasis on teaching and learning has continued.

The readings today combine to give us a pronounced sense of movement from introspection to rededication. In the Old Testament reading, God calls the people to declare a time of fasting and penitence: "Yet even now . . . return to me with all your heart, with fasting, with weeping, and with mourning; and rend your hearts and not your garments [Joel 2:12–13]." The prophet echoes God's call and summons the people sincerely to repent and trust in the One who abounds in steadfast love. Paul, in the Epistle, appeals to the Corinthian church to be reconciled to God now: "Behold, now is the acceptable time; behold, now is the day of salvation [2 Cor. 6:2]." The Gospel follows up the Old Testament reading with Jesus' teaching to the disciples about genuine fasting, prayer, and charity. In all these readings, the real treasure is found in one's relationship with God.

Set out today with the children on a lenten journey

from Ashes to Easter. Point out that it is a journey that helps us look into our hearts, repent of our sins, and rededicate ourselves to God at our Easter destination. At some distance from where you are having your conversation, place a round, liturgically colored "target" with an outer band of purple for Lent, an inner band of gray for Good Friday, and a center of gold for Easter. Invite one of the children to look through a pair of binoculars and identify what is seen. Share with them the meaning of the colors. If possible keep the "target" visible for the entire season of Lent.

Prayer: O God, I know you are with me every step of my journey from Ashes to Easter. Amen.

LENT 1

Purple Playdough

Lesson 1:   Genesis 2:4b–9, 15–17, 25—3:7
Lesson 2:   Romans 5:12–21
Gospel: Matthew 4:1–11

Theme: We are co-creators with God

Resource: Purple playdough. Here's an easy recipe for playdough: put 2 cups of flour and 1 cup of salt in a pan on the stove on medium high. Pour in 2 cups of boiling water containing purple food coloring, 1 tablespoon of alum, and 2 tablespoons of oil. Stir and remove from pan and knead.

Development: The readings today integrate well. The story of the creation of humankind is the focus of the Old Testament lesson that describes human beginnings and the separation that occurs when people disobey God. The Epistle lesson reminds us about

Adam's fall and how, through the grace of Jesus Christ, we are offered eternal salvation. The Gospel shows how Jesus, although tempted by the devil, does not sin like Adam. Jesus, who understands our need for help in times of temptation, is with us in our own "wilderness" experiences.

The common thread that I discern in these lessons is that, by God's grace, we are co-creators with the Creator. Fashioned in the image or likeness of God, we are called to a creative divine-human partnership that is confirmed by the Holy Spirit's invigorating, sustaining presence. God is with us! We are not alone in the daily creation of our lives.

Enable the children to experience that they are co-creators with God by giving each one a lump of freshly made purple (signifying Lent) playdough, and invite them literally to play with the dough for a minute. Indicate that in God's sight everyone is creative. Let them take the playdough home as a reminder of the day's theme on their journey toward Easter. Enjoy!

Prayer: Creator, it's great creating with you! Amen.

LENT 2

"We're Moving!"

Lesson 1:   Genesis 12:1–8
Lesson 2:   Romans 4:1–9, 13–17
Gospel: John 3:1–17

Theme: Traveling by faith
Resources: Four or five appropriately marked packing boxes

Development: The first lessons throughout Lent capture a sense of journey in which God calls people to new lands and new adventures. "Now God said to Abraham, 'Go from your country and your kindred and your father's house to the land that I will show you. And I will make of you a great nation, and I will bless you [Gen. 12:1–2].' " So begins today's Old Testament record of God's call to Abraham and Sarah to leave their home in the Tigris-Euphrates valley and travel to Canaan. A covenant is established between God and Abraham and his descendants.

Abraham and Sarah are cited as examples of faithful travelers in the Epistle lesson, and Paul points out that it is faith, not works of the law, that enables a relationship with God: "The promise to Abraham and Sarah and their descendants, that they should inherit the world, did not come through the law but through the righteousness of faith [Rom. 4:13]." The Gospel describes how Nicodemus comes to Jesus inquiring how to be born again.

Focus today on God's call to us to venture forth in faith. Tell the story of God's call to Abraham, especially noting his response: "So Abraham went, as God had told him [Gen. 12:4]." Point out that a great deal was expected of him: he had to leave everything and everyone. Use packing boxes marked "kitchen," "David's books," "Lindsey's toys," etc., to underline the idea of moving. Draw on the moving experiences of the children and ask them particularly to identify the feelings that they had in the course of moving. What stands out in my childhood memory is the phrase "We're moving!" Affirm that God calls each of us to a lifelong journey of faith.

Prayer: O God, help me to hear your call and travel by faith. Amen.

LENT 3

No Gain Without Pain

Lesson 1: Exodus 17:3–7
Lesson 2: Romans 5:1–11
Gospel: John 4:5–42

Theme: Suffering produces endurance
Resources: Track suit; muscle liniment

Development: We continue our lenten journey from Ashes to Easter with a look at the conditions or hardships we may encounter along the way. The Gospel is the story of Jesus' encounter with the woman at the well in Samaria. Jesus indicates to her that what she needs is the "living water" so that she may never thirst. The idea of thirst is also the focus of the Old Testament lesson in which the Israelites complain to Moses about the lack of water in the wilderness. The people ask Moses a revealing question: "Why did you bring us up out of Egypt, to kill us and our children and our cattle with thirst [Exod. 17:3]?" The Epistle addresses suffering and the nature of God's love: "Therefore, since we are justified by faith, we have peace with God through our Sovereign Jesus Christ. . . . We rejoice in our sufferings, knowing that suffering produces endurance, and endurance produces character, and character produces hope [Rom. 5:1, 3–4]."

Zero in on the theme that suffering produces endurance by wearing a track suit or similar clothing that conveys the idea of exercise. Express that just as a person stretches her or his muscles and occasionally feels sore, so we on our Christian journey, when we stretch our spiritual muscles, may experience some spiritual soreness. You may want to use a bottle of muscle liniment at this point. Explain that if we keep stretching regularly, we will be able to endure: if we stretch regularly in a spiritual sense, we'll be able to go the distance for God. Literally stretch as you are having your conversation with the children if you are able. You may want to invite someone to assist you. Just do what feels comfortable. Confirm that there is no gain without pain.

Prayer: O God, teach me your way that I may endure for you. Amen.

LENT 4

How to Choose a King

Lesson 1:   1 Samuel 16:1–18
Lesson 2:   Ephesians 5:8–14
Gospel: John 9:1–41

Theme: Samuel anoints David as king over Israel
Resource: "Anointing oil"

Development: The readings today present three possibilities for conversations with the children, all of which can be related to the lenten journey theme from Ashes to Easter. The first is from the Epistle lesson that begins "For once you were stumbling in the night, but now you are light in the Sovereign; walk as children of light [Eph. 5:8]." The point could be made that God's people are expected to live with openness. The second and third possibilities are related to the same theme of anointing. In the Gospel, Jesus heals the one born blind by an act of anointing: "Jesus spat on the ground and made clay of the spittle and anointed the blind person's eyes with the clay, saying 'Go, wash in the pool of Siloam.' . . . So the blind person went and washed and came back seeing [John 9:6–7]." On the Christian journey, we are healed by God's grace revealed in the Christ, whose name in Greek means anointed.

The third possibility emerges from the beautiful Old Testament story of how the prophet Samuel received a vision to go to Jesse's family to find a successor to Saul. "And God said: 'Arise, anoint [David]; for this is the one!' Then Samuel took the horn of oil, and anointed David in the midst of his brothers; and the Spirit of God came mightily upon David from that day forward [1 Sam. 16:12–13]." Invite someone to play the part of and dress as David to enter at the appropriate point in the action. Encourage the children to touch the oil as you begin, and actually anoint the forehead of the person playing David. Communicate the joyous connotation of this ritual of consecration. Assure the children that God has chosen and anointed each of them as a special person.

Prayer: God of all people, anoint me so that I can live for you. Amen.

LENT 5

Dry Bones

Lesson 1: Ezekiel 37:1–14
Lesson 2: Romans 8:6–19
Gospel: John 11:17–45

Theme: God restores the people
Resource: A human skeleton (or a dry bone)

Development: The theme of all three readings today is resurrection to newness of life. Paul, in his letter to the church at Rome, describes life in the Spirit: "To set the mind on the flesh is death, but to set the mind on the Spirit is life and peace [Rom. 8:6]." New life, then, is given to each one who permits the Spirit of God to dwell in them. The Gospel is the record of how Jesus raised Lazarus from the dead. Jesus states clearly to Martha that he is life: "I am the resurrection and the life; those who believe in me, though they die, yet shall they live, and whoever lives and believes in me shall never die [John 11:25–26]."

The Old Testament lesson is the incredible vision that Ezekiel has of God restoring the people of Israel. The faithful remnant in Babylonian captivity appeared to be dead and their God defeated. Ezekiel is set down in a valley full of dry bones, and God asks him: "O mortal, can these bones live [Ezek. 37:3]?" Ezekiel answers that only God knows and then prophesies as God commanded him. The bones come together with sinew and flesh and skin, and finally, God breathed life into the bones and "they lived, and stood upon their feet [Ezek. 37:10]."

Communicate this vision of Ezekiel's by using a human skeleton either upright on a frame or sitting on a chair. You may want to soften the impact of the skeleton, which can be quite upsetting for a child, by putting a toque on its head and a scarf around its neck. Read the story aloud with wonder and conviction so that the children can feel the breath of God restoring life to the dry bones! Underscore that it is God who breathes life into us on our journey, through the gracious Spirit of Jesus Christ who is the way, the truth, and the life!

Prayer: O Creator, breathe real life into me today. Amen.

Gladsad

Lesson 1: Isaiah 50:4–9a
Lesson 2: Philippians 2:5–11
Gospel: Matthew 26:14—27:66 (Passion Sunday)
  Matthew 21:1–11 (Palm Sunday)

Theme: Jesus' palm procession and passion
Resources: Palm branches for each child; thirty silver dollars

Development: Life on the Christian journey is a combination of joy and sadness, laughter and tears, ecstasy and pain. This Sunday presents a splendid opportunity to share this reality as we remember two prominent events on Jesus' journey: the palm procession into the city of Jerusalem and his passion. Although many traditions follow either the palm or the passion emphasis, my suggestion today is to pursue a dual direction with the children, using the two Gospel readings. With the exception of the Gospel readings appointed for today, the first and second lessons are the same and provide good background material. In the first lesson, the prophet Isaiah declares that God has supported him and will continue to protect him even against his enemy. The second lesson is an early Christian hymn in which Paul describes to the Philippians how Jesus humbled himself and was obedient to his death on the cross.

Give each child a "palm branch" as they gather, and begin with a jubilant procession of the palms. This act of participation will set the scene and mood for the dramatic contrast that will take place between Jesus' entrance into Jerusalem and the last Passover meal Jesus eats with his disciples. Invite the children, while holding the palm branches, to listen to the story of

Judas' betrayal of Jesus. Explain that the word passion comes from *passio,* which means "to suffer" (Matthew 26:14–30). Describe first the encounter between Judas and the high priests and then the meal. Use thirty silver dollars graphically to illustrate the amount paid to the chief priests. Enable the children to feel the joy and sadness of Jesus on his journey, and express how God was with Jesus all the time and is also with us always on our journey.

Prayer: O God, thanks for being with me when I'm glad and when I'm sad. Amen.

MAUNDY THURSDAY

Real Humility

Lesson 1:   Exodus 12:1–14
Lesson 2:   1 Corinthians 11:17–32
Gospel: John 13:1–17, 34

Theme: Jesus washes the disciples' feet
Resources: A basin; water; a towel

Development: All three readings for Maundy Thursday help us to gain a deep appreciation of the eucharist. In the Old Testament lesson, God instructs Israel on keeping the first Passover: an ancient meal, or seder, that recalled the story of the exodus of the Israelites from Egypt to the land of Canaan. This not only reflected their former slavery, but also praised God for their salvation. "This day shall be for you a memorial day, and you shall keep it as a feast to God; throughout your generations you shall observe it as an ordinance for ever [Exod. 12:14]." Paul, in the second lesson, writes to the Corinthians about the Last

Supper, which, like the seder, serves to remind those who participate in it of God's saving action: "For as often as you eat this bread and drink the cup, you proclaim the Sovereign's death until Christ comes [1 Cor. 11:26]."

The Gospel records how Jesus washed the disciples' feet before the Passover. Focus on Jesus' example of servanthood exemplified in his humble act of washing his followers' feet. This simple act surely stunned the disciples. Invite one of the children to wear sandals today, and actually wash her or his feet and dry them with a towel. Take extra care to prepare the children by talking about how one's feet got dirty from the dust on the road in Jesus' day. Make the point that we must follow the example of humility set by Jesus. The last verse of the Gospel puts humility in perspective: "A new commandment I give to you, that you love one another; even as I have loved you, that you also love one another [John 13:34]."

Prayer: Dear God, help me to love as you love. Amen.

GOOD FRIDAY

A Crown of Thorns

Lesson 1: Isaiah 52:13—53:12
Lesson 2: Hebrews 4:14–16; 5:7–9
Gospel: John 18:1—19:42

Theme: The suffering of Jesus
Resource: A crown of thorns

Development: Good Friday can be a positively powerful day in a child's spiritual development. We have traveled together through the purple of Lent and now pass through the gray of Good Friday on our way to the gold of Easter. There is no Easter without Good Friday! Passion/Palm Sunday's theme on "Gladsad" will have provided a good foundation for the conversation with the children today that focuses on the suffering and death of Jesus.

The prophet Isaiah, in the fourth servant song, describes the suffering servant who suffers and bears the sins of many: "This servant was wounded for our transgressions, was bruised for our iniquities, bore the chastisement that made us whole and the stripes by which we are healed [Isa. 53:5]." The Epistle reading states that Jesus "learned obedience through suffering; and being made perfect became the source of eternal salvation to all who obey [Heb. 5:8–9]." Jesus, by his suffering, identified with humanity. The long Gospel reading records Jesus' arrest, trial, and death.

In order to help the children grasp the essential meaning of Jesus' suffering for us and our salvation, use a crown of thorns. The Gospel describes the violence inflicted: "Then Pilate had Jesus scourged. And the soldiers plaited a crown of thorns, and put it on Jesus' head, and arrayed Jesus in a purple robe [John 19:1–2]." Plait or braid the thorns while you tell them about the sad events that took place on Good Friday. Assure them that it's all right to have sad feelings, especially if someone is suffering or dying, and that in our human suffering, God is always with us.

Prayer: Loving God, thank you for Jesus, who suffered for us all. Amen.

The Season of Easter

Hallelujah!

Lesson 1:   Acts 10:34–48
Lesson 2:   Colossians 3:1–11
Gospel: John 20:1–18

Theme: The resurrection of Jesus
Resource: A fresh gold-colored flower for each child

Development: Easter is the glorious destination of the lenten journey that began on Ash Wednesday. Purple has changed to gray and now to gold, signifying purity, perfection, and joy. Easter is a day for celebration and begins the season that proclaims Christ's eternal presence among us. The reality and mystery of God's love are to be experienced as the life and witness of the church unfold.

Ticket The Gospel lesson, in which the risen Christ appears to Mary Magdalene, is the real focus today and is supported by the other two lessons. The reading from the Acts of the Apostles records an early sermon preached by Peter about Jesus' life, death, and resurrection. Peter boldly proclaims the crucified and risen Christ. The second lesson addresses the matter of our new life in Christ that demands that we "seek the things that are above . . . and put on the new nature, which is being renewed in knowledge after the image of its creator [Col. 3:1, 10]."

Provide the environment really to celebrate Easter with genuine shouts and songs of praise and thanksgiving. If the children have been with you for the lenten journey, they'll be more than ready to shout "Hallelujah!" You may want to create a shout liturgy in which "Hallelujah" is the shouted response. In your conversation, tell the story of how Mary Magdalene goes to the tomb and how Jesus appeared to her. To mark this high festival and celebrate the new life in Christ, give each child a fresh gold-colored flower to take home to remind them in this season of God's saving action in Jesus Christ.

Prayer: Hallelujah! Jesus is risen! Amen.

EASTER 2

"To My Grandchildren . . ."

Lesson 1:   Acts 2:14a, 22–32
Lesson 2:   1 Peter 1:3–9
Gospel: John 20:19–31

Theme: The resurrection of Christ
Resource: A legal will form

Development: The resurrection of Christ is addressed from three perspectives in the readings. In the first lesson, Peter preaches a sermon to the people of Israel, stating emphatically that "God raised Jesus up, having loosed the pangs of death, because it was not possible for him to be held by it [Acts 2:24]." We are all witnesses, says Peter, of God's action in Christ. The risen Christ appears to Thomas in the Gospel, and the disciples are solidly bound together by their common conviction in the presence of the risen Christ. Not only is peace given to the disciples, but also the Holy Spirit. The second lesson, written by Peter, about two generations after the resurrection, to Christians in a time of persecution, sees the resurrection as central to the Christian faith. With joy he says: "Blessed be God the Father and Mother of our Sovereign Jesus Christ! By God's great mercy we have been born anew to a living hope through the resurrection of Jesus Christ from the dead, and to an inheritance which is imperishable, undefiled, and unfading, kept in heaven for you [1 Pet. 1:3–4]." Any one of these readings would be an excellent foundation on which to build a conversation.

Focus today on the theme of the resurrection as an assured inheritance. The readers of Peter's letter clearly understood that this new inheritance was beyond the often afflicted state of Canaan, the promised land God had given to Israel. This new inheritance was imperishable or enduring, undefiled or pure, and unfading or permanently bright. And it was in safekeeping for them. Communicate this good news by using a legal will form and express that just as a will outlines an inheritance, so we as God's people, by the resurrection of Christ, are promised by God's grace a wonderful eternal inheritance. You might want to invite a lawyer to assist you in the conversation today with the "children of promise."

Prayer: We praise you, O God of promise. Amen.

EASTER 3

"In the Breaking of Bread . . ."

Lesson 1: Acts 2:14a, 36–47
Lesson 2: 1 Peter 1:17–23
Gospel: Luke 24:13–35

Theme: Jesus meets two disciples on the road to Emmaus

Resource: A loaf of bread

Development: The Easter season continues with the conclusion of Peter's sermon in lesson one, in which he describes life in the early Christian community: "And they devoted themselves to the apostles' teaching and community life, to the breaking of bread and the prayers. . . . And all who believed were together and had all things in common. . . . And day by day, attending the temple together and breaking bread in their homes, they partook of food with glad and generous hearts, praising God and having favor with all the people [Acts 2:42, 44, 46–47]." When this first lesson is placed beside the Gospel, in which Jesus meets two disciples on the road to Emmaus, we discover that the disciples recognized who Jesus was in his teaching, the breaking of bread and prayers, the hallmark practices of the early church. "When he was at table with them, Jesus took the bread and blessed, and broke it, and gave it to them. And their eyes were opened and they recognized Jesus. . . . They said to each other, 'Did not our hearts burn within us while Jesus talked to us on the road and opened to us the scriptures [Luke 24:30–32]?' "

Convey briefly to the children the nature of the early Christian community's practices described in Acts, and tell the story of Jesus' resurrection appearance to the two disciples on the road to Emmaus. When you get to the table scene, break a loaf of bread to emphasize that marvelous moment of recognition. We, too, when we break the bread at the eucharist, recognize, or literally re-know, Jesus and his resurrected power and love.

Prayer: Eternal God, your Spirit is always with us. May we see you everywhere we go. Amen.

EASTER 4

"You Stiff-neckers!"

Lesson 1:　Acts 6:1–9; 7:2a, 51–56
Lesson 2:　1 Peter 2:19–25
Gospel:　John 10:1–10

Theme:　Openness and obedience to God's Spirit
Resource:　A heating pad

Development:　The Easter-season focus on life in the early church is evident in the first lesson, in which Stephen, full of the Holy Spirit, preaches: "Hear me, . . . you stiff-necked people, insensitive in heart and ears, you always resist the Holy Spirit. As your ancestors did, so do you [Acts 7:2, 51]." Help the children to grasp the meaning of the descriptive phrase "stiff-necked people" by using a heating pad placed on your neck as if it were stiff. Inquire whether any of them has ever had a stiff neck and how it felt. If you really do have a stiff neck today, it's providence! Explain that those who heard Stephen's sermon would be familiar with the phrase and would probably take serious offense to it. It is worth noting that Stephen, one of the first seven deacons, assistants to the twelve apostles, was the first martyr of the church, perhaps because he spoke so straightforwardly.

"Stiff-necked" is a metaphor for rebelliousness or unteachableness that is usually associated with the work of domestic animals. The ox, for example, stiffens its neck to refuse direction or turns its shoulder stubbornly when given the yoke. The term also was applied to Israel's attitude toward God in the wilderness. Stephen reminds the people that their ancestors were just like them in their resistance to the Holy Spirit by refusing to listen to the word of God formerly delivered to the prophets.

In contrast to the "stiff-necked" people whose heart and ears are insensitive, whose only concern is their own neck, the other two lessons present an image of Jesus the good shepherd, who openly cares and listens. It is Jesus' death and resurrection that ultimately and dramatically demonstrate that loving nature. Encourage the children to "loosen up" their necks and hearts to God's Spirit in order that "they may have life, and have it abundantly [John 10:10]."

Prayer: Loving God, help me to care with my heart and listen to you with my ears. Amen.

EASTER 5

"Jesus and the Living Stones"

Lesson 1:   Acts 17:1–15
Lesson 2:   1 Peter 2:1–10
Gospel: John 14:1–14

Theme: Christ is the living stone
Resources: Bricks (one to represent Christ the cornerstone and one for each child)

Development: Three good possibilities for conversations emerge from the readings today. The first reading records Paul in Thessalonica preaching that the risen Christ is indeed the Messiah. The Jews responded with resolute anger, and some claimed to the city authorities that "these people who have turned the world upside down have come here also, . . . and they are all acting against the decrees of Caesar, saying there is another ruler, Jesus [Acts 17:6–7]." The Gospel contains Jesus' well-known statement to Thomas: "I am the way, and the truth, and the life; no one comes to God, but by me [John 14:6]." Both of these readings provide graphic images, as does the second lesson, which describes Christ as the living stone.

Pursue the last option by building a corner out of bricks. Explain that Peter's letter was written to Christians who were being persecuted, and therefore welcomed his invitation: "Come to Christ, to that living stone, rejected by human beings but in God's sight chosen and precious; and like living stones be yourselves built into a spiritual house, to be a holy priesthood, to offer spiritual sacrifices acceptable to God through Jesus Christ [1 Pet. 2:4–5]." Christ, although once rejected by the builders, has now become the most important one, the precious cornerstone. Probe the notion that a stone can live. Place the "Christ cornerstone" in the corner and build a corner wall, using a brick for each child. Note that in so doing, one brick touches another and when we are joined to the living, resurrected Christ, we, too, will live.

Invite them to take a brick home as a tangible symbol of their special part in the spiritual house of "Jesus and the living stones."

Prayer: Creator of all, I want to build my life on Jesus Christ, the cornerstone. Amen.

EASTER 6

Here! There! Everywhere!

Lesson 1: Acts 17:22–31
Lesson 2: 1 Peter 3:8–22
Gospel: John 14:15–21

Theme: God is everywhere

Resources: A photograph of your church and of one or two others; photographs of various spaces, as described below; bristol board

Development: The conversation last week, on the fifth Sunday of Easter, ties in well with today's theme that God is everywhere and cannot be contained in holy buildings. At the Areopagus, a public forum in Athens, the intellectual and cultural center of the Greek world, Paul preaches: "People of Athens, I perceive that in every way you are very religious. For as I passed along, and observed the objects of your worship, I found also an altar with this inscription, 'To an unknown god.' What therefore you worship as unknown, this I proclaim to you. The God who made the world and everything in it, being Sovereign of heaven and earth, does not live in shrines made by humans [Acts 17:22–24]." Paul introduces them to the one true God revealed in Jesus Christ and indicates that the God he worships is present everywhere.

Remind the children of the "spiritual house" that they built last week with Christ as the cornerstone. Show a photo of your church and two other churches of different architecture, and indicate that indeed God is with you right now in your building and in other church buildings as well. Communicate that God, in a mysterious way, is present not only in our churches but everywhere by showing photos, posters, etc. of a variety of spaces, such as other communities, countries, streets, open spaces, the universe, a backyard, a schoolroom, a bedroom, a baseball field they play in. Newspapers and magazines are good resources. Use your imagination. You might find it helpful to place all the pictures on a large piece of bristol board. However you do it, convey that God is present everywhere.

Prayer: Thank you, O God, for being with us here in our church and home and school and everywhere! Amen.

EASTER 7 (ASCENSION)

You've Got the Power!

Lesson 1:   Acts 1:1–14
Lesson 2:   1 Peter 4:12–19
Gospel: John 17:1–11

Theme: God empowers us as messengers of good news
Resources: A large courier envelope or pouch; one small courier envelope for each child

Development: Last week, on the sixth Sunday of Easter, we noted that God is everywhere. In today's first lesson, the disciples are told by Jesus to "wait for the promise of God [Acts 1:4]," and they would "receive power when the Holy Spirit has come upon you; and you shall be my witnesses in Jerusalem and in all Judea and Samaria and to the end of the earth [Acts 1:8]." The disciples are to be sent out everywhere God is, filled with the power of the Spirit and the good news of the resurrection of Christ. They will be empowered by the eternally present Spirit. Just as "Jesus was lifted up, and carried on a cloud out of their sight [Acts 1:9]," so the disciples are to be "lifted up" to fulfill their ministry mandate.

Help the children to appreciate the incredible power of the Holy Spirit that can enable them to be witnesses where they live now and wherever they go in the name of Christ.

Illustrate this theme by comparing them to a personal messenger service for God sent to all people everywhere. Show them a large courier envelope or pouch containing smaller envelopes, and give one of the smaller envelopes to each child. Put your church's name and address on their envelope to indicate where they're from, and invite the children to tell where in the world they might imagine God sending them with the good news. Let them know that all God's people are asked to be messengers for God and that missionaries have a special role in this regard. If you have a missionary or missionaries associated with your church or denomination, highlight their ministry.

Prayer: Everywhere God, send us out today with your power. Amen.

The Season of Pentecost

Red Day

Lesson 1: Joel 2:28–32
Lesson 2: Acts 2:1–21
Gospel: John 20:19–23

Theme: The day of Pentecost

Resources: A piece of red cloth 1' wide by 6' long fastened to a piece of dowel 18" long, one for each child (too many is better than too few)

Development: Pentecost, like Easter, is a time for joyous celebration, expressed by the color red. This day starts a season that marks the beginning of the missionary life of the Christian church. An old thanksgiving festival or ritual that has its roots in the Jewish tradition, it marked the end of the spring grain harvest fifty days after the Passover. Similarly, we keep Pentecost (from the Greek *pente*, meaning fifty) fifty days after Easter. Today our covenant with God is reaffirmed as the Holy Spirit fills the apostles and empowers them to share the gospel with people of different languages.

Share with the children the drama and wonder of Luke's stirring account: "When the day of Pentecost had come, they were all together in one place. And suddenly a sound came from heaven like the rush of a mighty wind, and it filled all the house where they were sitting. And there appeared to them tongues as of fire, distributed and resting on each one of them. And they were all filled with the Holy Spirit and began to speak in other tongues, as the Spirit gave them utterance [Acts 2:1–4]." What an exciting spiritual experience to hand down to our children! I say experience because the passage lends itself to dancing of spirit and body. Give each child a piece of red cloth

about a foot wide and six feet long fastened to a piece
of dowel about 18 inches long. One can make wonderful shapes by swinging the dowel in a circular motion.
Lead a parade, accompanied by exuberant marching
music, around the sanctuary or outside, where the
children can freely wave their "Pentecost flags" and
truly celebrate or keep Pentecost.

Prayer: God of wind and fire, fill me with your Holy
Spirit on this red day. Amen.

· TRINITY SUNDAY

Go!

Lesson 1: Deuteronomy 4:32–40
Lesson 2: 2 Corinthians 13:5–14
Gospel: Matthew 28:16–20

Theme: The Trinity
Resource: A "Commission Scroll" on which the Great
Commission is printed

Development: Trinity Sunday falls immediately after
Pentecost and gives an overall perspective of God's
nature and action. In this regard, the Gospel and the
second lesson are particularly helpful. Matthew records how Jesus commissioned the disciples to make
disciples, to baptize, and to teach: "All authority in
heaven and on earth has been given to me. Go therefore and make disciples of all nations, baptizing them
in the name of God the Father and Mother and of
Jesus Christ the beloved Child of God and of the Holy
Spirit, teaching them to observe all that I have commanded you; and lo, I am with you always, to the
close of the age [Matt. 28:18–20]." Unroll the scroll on

which has been printed the Great Commission, and read it to the children with confidence and enthusiasm. Help them to understand by your reading that Jesus was calling the disciples to challenging tasks that they could accomplish in God's name.

Note particularly that Jesus instructs them to baptize in the name of the triune God: God the Father and Mother and of Jesus Christ the beloved Child of God and of the Holy Spirit. Briefly explain each of the three dimensions, and express the thought that in baptism, we pray that the one who is baptized may be blessed by the threefold fullness of God's grace.

Close today by praying together the "Trinity" blessing that Paul offered to the church at Corinth (2 Corinthians 13:14), which is used at the conclusion of worship in many traditions.

Prayer: The grace of the Sovereign Jesus Christ
and the love of God
and the communion of the Holy Spirit
be with you all. Amen.

PENTECOST 2

Listen and Do

Lesson 1:   Genesis 12:1–9
Lesson 2:   Romans 3:21–28
Gospel: Matthew 7:21–29

Theme: Building one's life on Christ, the firm foundation
Resources: Two "small" houses, described below; bricks and sand; water; hose with spray nozzle

Development: The Gospel today provides a superlative image to implant in the children's minds and hearts. Jesus communicates that a life must be built on the solid foundation ot God's love by telling the parable of a house built on rock and a house built on sand. If possible, tell this story outside so that the full impact of the parable may be experienced. There are only two responses to Jesus' words: one can hear them and do them, or one can hear them and not do them. "Every one then who hears these words of mine and does them will be like someone wise enough to build a house upon the rock; and the rain fell, and the floods came, and the winds blew and beat upon that house, but it did not fall, because it had been founded on the rock. And every one who hears these words of mine and does not do them will be like the fool who built a house upon the sand; and the rain fell, and the floods came, and the winds blew and beat against that house, and it fell; and great was the fall of it [Matt. 7:24–27]."

Set up two "small" houses: one solidly built on a brick foundation that can't possibly collapse and another flimsily built on a sand foundation (use about eight to ten inches of sand so that when the house tumbles, great will be the fall of it!) that definitely will collapse. Invite a carpenter to assist you in the preparation, if necessary. There is no need to be elaborate. A hose with a spray nozzle can be used effectively to show the rains and the floods. Tell the story with some exaggeration, as Jesus did. Encourage the children to be like those who are wise enough to build their lives on the solid foundation of Jesus Christ.

Prayer: Creator, help me to build my life on Jesus, the solid foundation. Amen.

A Supper with Sinners

Lesson 1: Genesis 22:1–18
Lesson 2: Romans 4:13–18
Gospel: Matthew 9:9–13

Theme: Jesus calls sinners
Resources: A person whose leg is in a cast; a pair of crutches

Development: Jesus constantly surprised his hearers by his actions and teachings. The Gospel offers one of those surprising moments, which occurred after the call of Matthew the tax collector. Matthew probably followed Jesus to his home in Capernaum, and there, with his disciples, Jesus had "supper with sinners," tax collectors who were despised and unpopular. The Pharisees saw this supper scene and were deeply disturbed that Jesus not only cared for sinners, but also sought them out and invited them to follow in God's way. Jesus did not condone, or even tolerate, the sinners' activities that broke the laws of the synagogue but indicates in his answer to the Pharisees' question to the disciples, "Why does your teacher eat with tax collectors and sinners?" that "those who are well have no need of a physician, but those who are sick. . . . For I came not to call the righteous, but sinners [Matt. 9:11–13]."

Introduce the setting today by telling the children of Matthew's response to Jesus' call to discipleship and how Jesus was having dinner with sinners when the Pharisees' question arose. Focus on their question and Jesus' answer by illustrating that a person who has a broken leg needs to see a doctor, not the person whose leg is all right. If there is a child or someone in your group with a broken leg, by all means involve the person. Otherwise, a pair of crutches can effectively communicate the idea. Close by indicating that God's message of salvation is for them and all people.

Prayer: God, help me to follow you day by day. Amen.

The Dynamic Dozen

Lesson 1:   Genesis 25:19–34
Lesson 2:   Romans 5:6–11
Gospel: Matthew 9:35—10:8

Theme: The twelve apostles
Resources: A dozen extra large eggs in an egg carton—hardboiled if you think safer; bristol board

Development: The Gospel's record of Jesus' appointment of the twelve apostles (disciples) follows up Trinity Sunday's conversation, which centered on the commissioning of the disciples to go and make disciples, baptize, and teach. Tell the children that Jesus called the twelve because of the great needs that people had. "And Jesus went about all the cities and villages, teaching in their synagogues and preaching the gospel of the realm, and healing every disease and every infirmity. When he saw the crowds, he had compassion for them, because they were harassed and helpless, like sheep without a shepherd. Then he said to his disciples, 'The harvest is plentiful, but the laborers are few; pray therefore to the God who gives the harvest to send out laborers into the harvest [Matt. 9:35–38].' "

Explain that the word apostle is derived from the Greek *apostolos*, to send out, and denotes in the Christian setting a commissioned messenger or ambassador or missionary of the Gospel. As Jesus was sent by God, so he sends out the apostles to continue his mission. The chosen twelve were "the dynamic dozen" who turned the world upside down, proclaiming salvation through Christ. Show the children the dozen extra large eggs on which the apostles' names (Peter, Andrew, James Z, John, Philip, Bartholomew, Thomas, Matthew, James A, Thaddeus, Simon, Judas) have been printed. If you have a large group of children, they may not all be able to get close enough to read the relatively small printing on the eggs (especially Bartholomew). In this case, print the numbers from 1 through 12 on the eggs and print the corresponding numbers and names on a piece of bristol board. Conclude by indicating that just as Jesus chose the twelve, so he chooses us for dynamic ministry now.

Prayer: O God, in love you have called me by name and I will follow you. Amen.

A Very, Very Long Ladder!

Lesson 1:   Genesis 28:10–17
Lesson 2:   Romans 5:12–19
Gospel: Matthew 10:24–33

Theme: Jacob's dream of a ladder to heaven
Resource: A long ladder

Development: Two excellent possibilities for the conversation themes are presented in the readings. One is the idea that we need not fear anything or anyone because we are truly valued and cherished by God: "Even the hairs of your head are all numbered [Matt. 10:30]." The average person has about 120,000 head hairs (some have not been so generously blessed). You could develop this theme by making a rough count of the number of hairs on one child's head and perhaps looking at a single hair through a microscope.

The other possibility is to focus on the Old Testament's record of Jacob's dream: "And he dreamed that there was a ladder set up on the earth, and the top of it reached to heaven; and behold, the angels of God were ascending and descending on it! And behold, God stood above it [Gen. 28:12–13]." Set against a wall a ladder that is long enough to give the children a distinct sense of "going to heaven." Begin by telling them that everybody has three or four dreams every night and that this story is about a happy dream that Jacob had many years ago. Read the story well; try to communicate that for Jacob, it was a vision of hope. Really enable the children to dream! Close today by singing three verses (adapted) of the old spiritual "We Are Climbing Jacob's Ladder." Sing the first and second verses quietly while seated and then stand to sing the last verse joyfully.

Prayer: 1. We are climbing Jacob's ladder (repeat twice)
Children of the cross.
2. Every rung goes higher, higher (repeat twice)
Children of the cross.
3. Rise, shine, give God glory! (repeat twice)
Children of the cross.

"God's Glasses"

Lesson 1: Genesis 32:22–32
Lesson 2: Romans 6:3–11
Gospel: Matthew 10:34–42

Theme: Being a disciple of Jesus
Resource: A pair of eyeglasses

Development: The readings today present two possibilities, the first of which is the Old Testament account of how Jacob wrestled with a man until dawn. The outcome of Jacob's experience was that he had "seen God face to face, and yet my life is preserved [Gen. 32:30]." The other possibility, and the one I would suggest, is to focus on the Gospel, which considers what it means to be Jesus' disciple. The passage may be a little obscure for the children, and you will have to take extra care in discerning what precisely you want to convey.

Ask the children what they think a disciple is. Most children have a fair understanding of one who is a learner or pupil, or one who accepts a given doctrine or teacher. Solidify their thinking by pointing out that a disciple of Jesus is a person who regards Jesus as teacher and is committed to following only him. This is the real thrust of the Gospel. There must be no rivals: "Whoever loves father or mother more than me is not worthy of me [Matt. 10:37]."

Paul affirms this close connection between Jesus and a disciple when he says: "We were buried therefore with Christ by baptism into death, so that as Christ was raised from the dead by the glory of God the Father and Mother, we too might walk in newness of life [Rom. 6:4]." Jesus' disciples, in a spirit of total commitment, take up their crosses and follow. Use a pair of eyeglasses to communicate that being a disciple is like seeing all our lives through "God's glasses." We see life as God sees it: ourselves, our families, our school, our town or city, our church, our country, our world. Encourage them to be true disciples of Jesus and see everything this week through "God's glasses."

Prayer: Dear God, I want to be Jesus' disciple. Help me to see as you see. Amen.

PENTECOST 7

"The Yoke's on You"

Lesson 1:   Exodus 1:6–14, 22—2:10
Lesson 2:   Romans 7:14–25a
Gospel: Matthew 11:25–30

Theme: Living with Jesus
Resource: A double wooden yoke

Development: What a tremendous invitation Jesus gives in the Gospel: "Come to me, all who labor and are heavy laden, and I will give you rest. Take my yoke upon you, and learn from me; for I am gentle and lowly in heart, and you will find rest for your souls. For my yoke is easy, and my burden is light [Matt. 11:28–30]." Here is good news for all people, including children, who from time to time carry heavy burdens and seek rest and refreshment and peace.

To illustrate the statement of Jesus, demonstrate the use of a double wooden yoke—one side for Jesus and one side for us. Explain that Jesus probably had made many yokes with his carpenter father, Joseph. A yoke is a wooden frame placed over the necks of two draft animals, for example, oxen, joining them so that they can work together. The rabbis understood religion as the "yoke of the law," and the Pharisees and scribes placed this heavy burden of the law on the people. Jesus now invites the people to exchange the yoke of the law for his yoke of faith and love. When people are yoked to Christ, even though Christ's yoke is demanding and requires dedicated effort, they are blessed with rest.

Alan T. Dale's paraphrase of this passage in *New World: The Heart of the New Testament in Plain English* (page 85) is most enlightening: "Come here to me all you who are tired with hard work, I will put new life into you. Let me give you a hand and show you how to live. I'll go your pace and see you through—and I'll give you the secret of the quiet mind. Pulling with me is easy, the load with my help is light." Encourage the children to be yoked to Christ and to pull together.

Prayer: Thank you, O God, for being with me. Pulling with you is easy and the load with your help is light. Amen.

PENTECOST 8

"Love Seeds"

Lesson 1:   Exodus 2:11–22
Lesson 2:   Romans 8:9–17
Gospel: Matthew 13:1-9, 18–23

Theme: Hearing and doing the word of God
Resources: A small sandbox filled with soil; packages of "love seeds"

Development: The word parable is derived from the Greek *para*, which means "beside," and *ballo*, which means "to throw." Parable, then, literally means "to throw alongside." The Gospel contains Jesus' outstanding parable of the sower that he throws alongside the point he wants to make: hear and understand and do the word of God and your life will bear much fruit.

Graphically demonstrate the parable by using a small sandbox filled with soil. Create a path and discernible sections for rocky ground, thorny ground, and good soil. For clarity, you may wish to identify these sections in some way, such as by a little flag. Tell the story using imaginary seeds, and help the children to see in their mind's eye the birds devouring the seed or the thorns choking the life out of the plants, etc. Don't be afraid to exaggerate. Children love it. Let Jesus' explanation of the parable enable them to appreciate it at their level of understanding.

Give each child a small package of "love seeds" to take home as a reminder that God truly wants to plant the seeds of love in them to grow and produce much fruit.

Prayer: O God, plant your "seeds of love" in me so I can be fruitful for you. Amen.

PENTECOST 9

Tomorrow

Lesson 1: Exodus 3:1–12
Lesson 2: Romans 8:18–25
Gospel: Matthew 13:24–30, 36–43

Theme: Hope

Resources: A quarter, a newspaper weather forecast

Development: There are several directions in which one could go with the conversation today. The Old Testament lesson records the story of Moses witnessing the burning bush that was not consumed, how God delivered the people of Israel "out of the hand of the Egyptians" and brought them to "a land flowing with milk and honey [Exod. 3:8]," and how Moses was sent to Pharaoh. The Gospel is Jesus' parable of the weeds.

The Epistle lesson focuses on hope, and I would pursue this direction. Paul says: "I consider that the sufferings of this present time are not worth comparing with the glory that is to be revealed to us [Rom. 8:18]." He understands that the whole creation, as well as the children of God, is groaning for redemption, and that it is hope that sustains the people in their suffering. There will be a glorious day beyond what we could ever imagine!

Explore hope with the children by first pointing out that, as Paul warns, "hope that is seen is not hope. For who hopes for what is already seen [Rom. 8:24]?" and then showing a quarter in your open hand. One does not hope for a quarter that one sees! Then explain that Paul's hope for a glorious tomorrow is like tomorrow's weather forecast that might be found in a newspaper. Assure the children that in God's love, the best is yet to come!

Prayer: God of all time, I'm looking forward to tomorrow with you. Amen.

The Precious Pearl

Lesson 1: Exodus 3:13–20
Lesson 2: Romans 8:26–30
Gospel: Matthew 13:44–52

Theme: The realm of heaven

Resources: A jewelry box filled with "inexpensive pearls"; a jewel case with one "valuable"-appearing pearl

Development: What is the realm of heaven really like? Jesus addresses this question in the Gospel by telling three parables: the parable of the hidden treasure, the parable of the pearl, and the parable of the net. Use the first two today because they complement each other so well, and leave the third for another time.

"The realm of heaven is like treasure hidden in a field, which someone found and covered up; then in joy the finder goes and sells everything and buys that field [Matt. 13:44]." The realm of heaven often takes us by surprise. The person who uncovered the treasure wasn't looking for it, but when the discovery was made recognized its true value. So it is with the realm. When we discover the gospel, we know that we have found the real treasure.

"Again, the realm of heaven is like a merchant in search of fine pearls, who, on finding one pearl of great value, went and sold everything and bought it [Matt. 13:45–46]." To live in the realm of heaven is really to live!

Communicate this latter parable by using a common jewelry box filled with "inexpensive pearls" (costume jewelry will do) and an exquisite jewel case containing one valuable-appearing pearl. The merchant in the parable was searching for fine pearls and knew the value of them. So his action in selling all the others to purchase the precious pearl signifies that God's realm is so desirable that one will give everything in exchange for its possession. The result for the person in each parable is a sense of true joy that is found in Christ.

Prayer: O God, how wonderful your realm is! Amen.

PENTECOST 11

Inseparable!

Lesson 1: Exodus 12:1–14
Lesson 2: Romans 8:31–39
Gospel: Matthew 14:13–21

Theme: Nothing can separate us from God's love
Resources: A kite; kite string

Development: The spirit of Pentecost is clearly evident in the second lesson and Gospel. The latter is the wonderful story of Jesus feeding the five thousand: "Then he ordered the crowds to sit down on the grass; and taking the five loaves and the two fish he looked up to heaven, and blessed, and broke and gave the loaves to the disciples, and the disciples gave them to the crowds. . . . And they took up twelve baskets full of the broken pieces left over. And those who ate were about five thousand men, besides women and children [Matt. 14:19–21]."

In the Epistle, Paul sounds a note of hope to the early Christians: "Who shall separate us from the love of Christ? Shall tribulation, or distress, or persecution, or famine, or nakedness, or peril, or sword? . . . No, in all these things we are more than conquerers through the one who loved us. For I am sure that neither death, nor life, nor angels, nor principalities, nor things present, nor things to come, nor powers, nor height, nor depth, nor anything else in all creation, will be able to separate us from the love of God in Christ Jesus our Sovereign [Rom. 8:35, 37–39]."

Inspire the children with this truth! If it's a windy day, go fly a kite with them as a parable of the reality that nothing whatsoever can separate them from God's love in Christ. If you are unable to be outside on this occasion, why not suspend the kite from the ceiling to give them a simulated feeling of kite-flying. Let the one firmly holding the string signify Jesus, the unbreakable string, the connecting line of love, and the kite, the child. Let the freeing experience of kite-flying speak for itself without a whole lot of explanation. When each of us is connected to God in love, we are inseparable! Have fun in the spirit of hope!

Prayer: Thank you, O God, for your love that will never let me go. And let me really fly! Amen.

PENTECOST 12

Shh . . . It's Quiet Time

Lesson 1: Exodus 14:19–31
Lesson 2: Romans 9:1–5
Gospel: Matthew 14:22–33

Theme: Jesus praying alone
Resources: An adult-size rocking chair; a child-size rocking chair

Development: Two well-known Bible stories are found in the lessons today. The Old Testament reading recalls how Moses, under God's direction, led the people of Israel out of the hands of the Egyptians. The Gospel tells how Jesus walked on the water. Both stories certainly have much to offer, but my theological and practical difficulties with them prompt me to take another course in developing a conversation with the children.

Focus on the example set by Jesus to spend time quietly alone. Matthew records Jesus' action quite simply: "Then Jesus made the disciples get into the boat and go before him to the other side, while he dismissed the crowds. And after he had dismissed the crowds, he went up on the mountain by himself to pray [Matt. 14:22–23]." Jesus must have been nearly exhausted preaching, teaching, and healing. But he recognized his own need to have time apart to pray, to reconnect personally with God, to put things in perspective and be spiritually and physically refreshed. Children, too, need to learn early in their lives the necessity and the benefits of cultivating a daily quiet time.

Sit in a large rocking chair and impart this fundamental aspect of good spiritual practice by telling the children how Jesus went up on the mountain to pray. Invite one of the children to sit in the small rocking chair beside you, and indicate that all people need to take time each day to be alone with God to pray, read the Bible, and meditate. Give them a little direction about where, how much time, and what to read, and encourage them to have a quiet time every day this week.

Prayer: Dear God, help me to have a quiet time every day to keep in touch with you. Amen.

"God's Listening"

Lesson 1: Exodus 16:2–15
Lesson 2: Romans 11:13–16, 29–32
Gospel: Matthew 15:21–28

Theme: God listens
Resource: A large papier-mâché ear, or an ear cut out of bristol board

Development: The Old Testament lesson and the Gospel both reveal that God listens. In the former, Moses and Aaron receive the complaints of the people of Israel in the wilderness: "Would that we had died by the hand of God in the land of Egypt, when we sat by the fleshpots and ate bread to the full; for you have brought us out into this wilderness to kill this whole assembly with hunger [Exod. 16:3]." These complaints were really leveled at God, who hears them and responds by providing food. In the Gospel, Matthew tells the story of Jesus and the Canaanite woman who comes seeking mercy on her daughter, who is severely possessed by a demon. The disciples begged Jesus to send her away but she persisted, and Jesus said to her: " 'O woman, great is your faith! Be it done for you as you desire.' And her daughter was healed instantly [Matt. 15:28]."

God listens! Enable the children to grasp this essential nature of God by using a larger-than-life ear while telling one or both of the stories. A papier-mâché ear works well or an ear cut out of a piece of bristol board. The important point to convey is that God listens, not to personify God with a big ear! Ask the children what they pray to God, and listen attentively to their responses. In a real way you are a model of God's listening. Assure the children that God listens to us always and everywhere. God hears our complaints as reflected in the Old Testament story. God hears our persistent and earnest prayers for ourselves or others, as the Canaanite woman recognized. God listens to us when we express our fears, our thanks, our love, and our hopes.

Encourage them to remember that we can trust God to listen to our prayers today and every day.

Prayer: O God, thank you for hearing me now as I pray. Amen.

PENTECOST 14

"I Declare . . . !"

Lesson 1: Exodus 17:1–17
Lesson 2: Romans 11:33–36
Gospel: Matthew 16:13–20

Theme: Peter declares his faith in Christ
Resources: A copy of the vows used in confirmation; a copy of the United Nations Declaration of Human Rights

Development: The encounter of Jesus and his disciples at Caesarea Philippi marks a critical moment in the disciples' faith development. Jesus gently pressed them to declare their own belief, and it was Simon Peter who replied: "You are the Christ, the Child of the Living God [Matt. 16:16]."

Having heard Peter's declaration of faith, Jesus responded: "Blessed are you, Simon Bar-Jona! For flesh and blood has not revealed this to you, but God my Father and Mother who is in heaven. And I tell you, you are Peter, and on this rock I will build my church

[Matt. 16:17–18]." The faith of Peter in Christ and the faith of others who believe similarly will combine to be the embodiment of the church. This is good heavy theology for adults and children alike.

Children will at least have heard the word declaration. Ask them what they think it means, and help them to understand it as a clear statement of what is believed, for example, by a person or a country. You may want to refer to the United Nations Declaration of Human Rights or, if you live in the United States, the Declaration of Independence. Tell the story of Peter declaring his faith in Jesus and how it is important for each of us to declare our faith too. Illustrate this by directing their attention to the "declaration of faith" made in confirmation or church membership. Why not plan to welcome new members on this Sunday so that the children will witness faith being openly declared and the new believers received into the church fellowship, the body of Christ.

Remind the children that they don't have to get older to believe, and encourage them to declare their faith now.

Prayer: O loving God, with Peter I declare you are the Christ. Amen.

PENTECOST 15

"Cookie Cutter Kids"

Lesson 1:   Exodus 19:1–9
Lesson 2:   Romans 12:1–13
Gospel: Matthew 16:21–28

Theme: Offering one's self to God

Resources: Playdough, a person-shaped cookie cutter

Development: Again this Sunday the readings offer two directions for the conversation with the children. In the Gospel, Jesus tells the disciples what lies ahead and what his future will mean for them. He describes what true discipleship is like: "If any would come after me, let them deny themselves and take up their crosses and follow me. For those who would save their lives will lose them, and those who lose their lives for my sake will find them. For what is one profited, if one gains the whole world and forfeits one's life [Matt. 16:24–26]?"

The second direction, and the one I would take, is found in the Epistle lesson, in which Paul writes to the Roman Christians: "Present your bodies as a living sacrifice, holy and acceptable to God, which is your spiritual worship. Do not be conformed to this world but be transformed by the renewal of your mind, that you may prove what is the will of God, what is good and acceptable and perfect [Rom. 12:1–2]." Children need to hear that God is with them to help them deal with the pressures to conform to the standards and wishes of others and that God expects them truly and honorably to offer their whole selves as a living holy sacrifice or offering. Share with the children these thoughts, and illustrate the idea of conformity by rolling out some playdough (red if you want to make it liturgically colored for Pentecost) and cutting outlines with a person-shaped cookie cutter. Indicate that God created each of them not to be exactly like others, but to be, by God's love, themselves!

Prayer: Creator of all, thank you for creating only one of me. Help me each day by your love really to be me. Amen.

The Dynamic Difference

Lesson 1: Exodus 19:16–24
Lesson 2: Romans 13:1–10
Gospel: Matthew 18:15–20

Theme: The dynamic presence of God
Resources: Three adjustable desk lamps; a four-outlet electrical strip; ice cubes in a glass; a table

Development: In the Gospel lesson today, Jesus responds to a question from the disciples, stating the practice the church is to follow if your neighbor sins against you. The lesson offers three possibilities for your conversation with the children. One could zero in on the theme of listening being essential to interpersonal relationships with the community of Christ.

Second, there is the opportunity to center on forgiveness and reconciliation within the Christian family, with a view to Jesus' promise that "whatever you bind on earth shall be bound in heaven, and whatever you loose on earth shall be loosed in heaven [Matt. 18:18]."

The third possibility, and the one I would choose, is to consider the last verse of the passage, which states that God is dynamically present among God's people when they gather: "For where two or three are gathered in my name, there am I in the midst of them [Matt. 18:20]." Explore this theme with the children by reminding them of God's presence with you all today. Explain that when we combine God's energy flowing through us, we are able to do great things for God, greater than we would be able to do individually. Illustrate this truth by turning on a desk lamp that is plugged into a four-outlet electrical strip and focusing the lamp on a glass of ice cubes. Note that the heat from the lamp does indeed melt the ice cubes. Then repeat, using two additional lamps, and observe with the children "the dynamic difference" that takes place when three lamps are combined in the common purpose of melting the ice cubes. A quick rehearsal may be beneficial, especially in regard to timing. My ice cubes seemed somewhat reluctant to melt!

Prayer: Ever-present God, thanks for making things really happen when we gather in your name. Amen.

PENTECOST 17

70 × 7

Lesson 1: Exodus 20:1–20
Lesson 2: Romans 14:5–12
Gospel: Matthew 18:21–35

Theme: Forgiveness

Resources: Seventy pages of newsprint, on each of which "I forgive you" is printed seven times

Development: The readings for this Sunday provide several opportunities for your conversation with the children. The first lesson records the ten commandments, and the second lesson recalls how Paul appeals to the Christians at Rome not to pass judgment on one another. The Gospel that follows tells how Jesus compared the realm of heaven to a king who wished to settle accounts with his servants.

The story Jesus relates arises out of a question posed to Jesus by Peter: " 'My Sovereign, how often shall my brother and sister sin against me, and I forgive them? As many as seven times?' Jesus answered, 'I do not say to you seven times, but seventy times seven [Matt. 18:21–22].' " Rather than tell the story about the king and his servants today, pursue the far-reaching implications of these two verses that center on the meaning of forgiveness. Peter was willing to forgive—even seven times! But Jesus teaches him that true forgiveness knows no limit by multiplying by seventy the number of times Peter thought it more than reasonable to forgive.

Follow Jesus' example and exaggerate to make the point by using seventy pages of newsprint on each of which "I forgive you" is printed seven times. Relate the story and turn the pages one by one. The first two or three pages you may want to read all seven "I forgive you" statements, but in subsequent pages, one "I forgive you" will be adequate. Don't be surprised if the children join you in saying "I forgive you." Jesus wants us to forgive a lot!

Prayer: Forgiving God, help me in your name to forgive. Amen.

PENTECOST 18

The God Squad

Lesson 1: Exodus 32:1–14
Lesson 2: Philippians 1:1–11, 19–27
Gospel: Matthew 20:1–16

Theme: Partnership in the gospel
Resources: A team T-shirt; a T-shirt with "The God Squad" printed on it

Development: Paul's fondness for the Philippians is evident in the Epistle reading today: "I thank my God in all my remembrance of you, always in every prayer of mine for you all making my prayer with joy, thankful for your partnership in the gospel from the first day until now [Phil. 1:3–5]." One of the key phrases in these verses is "partnership in the gospel."

Explore with the children the meaning of this phrase by asking them first what a partner is. Listen to their answers and, if you wish, record them on newsprint. Enable them to understand that a partner is someone who shares, such as a partner in a game. Hold up a team T-shirt to convey that when several people share together, they, too, are partners. Explain that when we love God, it is as if we and God are partners and that when many people love God in one place, like the church, we are partners on God's team. At this point uncover a T-shirt you are wearing on which is printed "The God Squad." Indicate that Paul felt that he was a member of God's team in Philippi. Reflect with them on what it means to be partners with God in your setting, using a sports team image. You might chat about cooperation, caring, loyalty, enthusiasm, practicing, giving your best to God. Help them to feel that they play an important role on "The God Squad" in your church. 10—11—87

Prayer: O God, it's fun being a partner with you. Amen.

PENTECOST 19

God at Work

Lesson 1:   Exodus 33:12–23
Lesson 2:   Philippians 2:1–13
Gospel: Matthew 21:28–32

Theme: God is at work in us

Resources: Large "GOD AT WORK" signs; a button with "GOD AT WORK" printed on it for each child

Development: The Epistle reading from Philippians continues this Sunday with Paul's reflection on Christ's example of humility and obedience. Paul urges a full caring spirit of partnership among them: "So if there is any encouragement in Christ, any incentive of love, any participation in the Spirit, any affection and sympathy, complete my joy by being of the same mind, having the same love, being in full accord and of one mind [Phil. 2:1–2]." Even though Paul will no longer be with them, he affirms the action of God among them: "Therefore, my beloved, as you have always obeyed, so now, not only as in my presence but much more in my absence, work out your own salvation with fear and trembling; for God is at work in you, both to will and to work for God's good pleasure [Phil. 2:12–13]."

Prepare for the conversation this morning by having large "GOD AT WORK" signs visibly placed at all entrances to the church building or where you gather. Inquire whether the children noticed something new today when they came in. Convey to them that "God is at work" in them creating, inspiring, and loving just as God was at work in the early Christians at Philippi. Give each one of them a button with "GOD AT WORK" printed on it. You may want to have a few extra buttons to give to the adults who have button collections. Buttons may be cut out of craft paper, but my experience is that there is nothing like the real thing.

Prayer: O God, it's great to know you're at work in me! Amen.

Nobody's Perfect!

Lesson 1: Numbers 27:12–23
Lesson 2: Philippians 3:12–21
Gospel: Matthew 21:33–43

Theme: Perfection
Resource: A baseball bat

Development: Paul continues his warm encouragement of his Christian friends at Philippi in this Sunday's Epistle reading by offering them a superb image of his own perspective in the faith: "Not that I have already obtained true righteousness or am already perfect; but I press on to make it my own, because I have been taken hold of by Christ Jesus. Sisters and brothers, I do not consider that I have made it on my own; but one thing I do, forgetting what lies behind and straining forward to what lies ahead, I press on toward the goal for the prize of the upward call of God in Christ Jesus [Phil. 3:12–14]."

Focus today on Paul's introductory confession that he does not consider himself to be perfect. Many children face high expectations of parents and teachers and athletic coaches, etc., and often "perfection" is sought with a definite price to pay. Perfection, however, must be viewed in perspective. A student of ballet knows only too well that perfection is the goal but also knows that toward that end, mistakes will be made and need to be corrected. Children need to hear, particularly from the community of faith, that nobody's perfect. Explore this theme with them by using a baseball bat and pretend swinging. Indicate that a batter never hits the ball all the time. Even the great sluggers, like Mickey Mantle, missed and struck out. It only takes a major league batting average of

.300 to be admitted to the Baseball Hall of Fame. Encourage them "to press on toward the goal for the prize of the upward call of God in Christ Jesus [Phil. 3:14]" with the confidence that God knows we'll fail from time to time and that that's all right. Nobody's perfect!

Prayer: Loving God, I know if I swing and miss you'll understand. Amen.

PENTECOST 21

"Dear . . ."

Lesson 1:   Deuteronomy 34:1–12
Lesson 2:   Philippians 4:1–9
Gospel: Matthew 22:1–14

Theme: Letters
Resources: A table; paper and pen

Development: This Sunday's Epistle lesson, the last from a series on Philippians, provides an excellent opportunity to reflect with the children about letters and letter-writing and letter-reading. We sometimes forget that a major part of the New Testament is in the style of a letter.

Sit at a table today with paper and pen, and pretend you are Paul writing the last verse of the passage. Stay in character and read Philippians 4:1–9. You might want to extend the reading to verse 23 because the latter verses read like a thank-you note and contain Paul's final greetings. Explain that Paul was writing to his friends at Philippi to tell them how he felt toward them and what his hopes were for them: "So then my sisters and brothers, how dear you are to me and how

I miss you! How happy you make me, and how proud I am of you! This then . . . is how you should stand firm in your life." Paul wanted to make sure that his friends continued to grow in faith.

Chat with the children informally about letters, and invite them to share with you what they like best about sending and receiving them. For a child, to receive a letter addressed to her or him is an event. Why not follow up your discussion with them by sending each one a brief letter in the mail this week. Surprise them! It won't take much time and your letter may be treasured for a lifetime.

Prayer: Dear God, I love you. Amen.

PENTECOST 22

A Trick Question

Lesson 1:   Ruth 1:1–19a
Lesson 2:   1 Thessalonians 1:1–10
Gospel: Matthew 22:15–22

Theme: Be wise
Resource: A silver dollar, or large coin

Development: This Sunday's Gospel, which records Jesus' response to the Pharisees' question about paying taxes to Caesar, is worth exploring with the children. The Pharisees asked Jesus a trick question: "Teacher, we know that you are true, and teach the way of God truthfully, and court no one's favor; for you do not regard a person's status. Tell us, then, what you think. Is it lawful to pay taxes to Caesar, or not [Matt. 22:16–17]?" They tried to catch Jesus off guard with a question so that no matter how he answered, he would offend either the Roman rulers or the religious establishment. Instead, Jesus recognized their malice and asked a question in return: "Why put me to the test, you hypocrites? Show me the money for the tax [Matt. 22:18–19]."

Share the first part of the encounter with the children, and ask them if they've ever been asked a trick question or have been tricked. Convey that God wants us to be wise in judging those who have good intentions and those who do not. Being "street-wise" for God's sake is important.

Then tell how Jesus answered the Pharisees' trick question, using a silver dollar or a large coin with your "national" inscription on it to make the point. Express that it is appropriate for us to "render therefore to Caesar the things that are Caesar's, and to God the things that are God's [Matt. 22:21]."

Prayer: O God, thanks for being with me, especially when someone's trying to trick me. Amen.

PENTECOST 23

The Big Two

Lesson 1: Ruth 2:1–13
Lesson 2: 1 Thessalonians 2:1–8
Gospel: Matthew 22:34–46

Theme: The two great commandments
Resources: Newsprint; marker

Development: Have some fun with the Gospel today. Matthew records how one of the Pharisees, a lawyer, tested Jesus with a question: " 'Teacher, which is the great commandment in the law?' And Jesus said to him, 'You shall love the Sovereign your God with all your heart, and with all your soul, and with all your mind. This is the great and first commandment. And a second is like it, You shall love your neighbor as yourself. On these two commandments depend all the law and the prophets [Matt. 22:36–40].' "

Play a game of charades with the children to give variety of presentation and securely implant the two commandments. Younger children may need more assistance, especially if they've never played the game before. Explain that you want to tell them about "The Big Two" commandments, and then act them out and see if they can determine what the commandments are. A quick run-through at home or with friends (they're usually pretty good critics) will help you to iron out some of the rough spots. When they've got the answers—"Love God" and "Love your neighbor as yourself"—write them on newsprint. And by the way, communicating the idea of neighbor can be a little tricky. Enjoy!

Prayer: Loving God, help me to love you and my neighbor. Amen.

PENTECOST 24

Practice What You Preach

Lesson 1:   Ruth 4:7–17
Lesson 2:   1 Thessalonians 2:9–13, 17–20
Gospel: Matthew 23:1–12

Theme: God, the true teacher
Resource: An academic robe

Development: In the Gospel, Jesus talks to the disciples about who their true teacher is. He warns them that "the scribes and the Pharisees sit on Moses' seat; so practice and observe whatever they tell you, but not what they do; for they preach, but do not practice [Matt. 23:2–3]." Obey and follow the good theory they impart to you, but don't imitate their actions. Jesus goes on to describe those who practice but do not preach: "They bind heavy burdens, hard to bear, and lay them on people's shoulders; but they themselves will not move them with their finger. They do all their deeds to be seen by others; for they make their phylacteries broad and their fringes long, and they love the place of honor at feasts and the best seats in the synagogues, and salutations in the market places, and being called rabbi by everyone [Matt. 23:4–7]."

Tell the children that God is the only true teacher and that all true learning comes from God. Talk to them about the bad example set by the scribes and the Pharisees, who heartlessly required others to obey the heavy demands of the law while they did not, and who sought recognition rather than humility. Wear an academic gown to illustrate the idea of recognition. The children may be able to point to experiences in their own lives about this regard.

Help them to understand that teachers and learners alike must practice what they preach. Children generally have a fairly accurate judgment about this and know when a teacher talks of fairness but acts unfairly. Encourage them to practice what they preach this week.

Prayer: O God, our true teacher, help me to practice what I preach. Amen.

Be Prepared!

Lesson 1: Amos 5:18–24
Lesson 2: 1 Thessalonians 4:13–18
Gospel: Matthew 25:1–13

Theme: Be prepared
Resources: An oil lamp; a flask of oil; a flashlight; a poncho

Development: A diverse variety of themes emerges from the readings this Sunday. In the first lesson, Amos announces that the day of God will be a day of judgment on which justice will "roll down like waters, and righteousness like an everflowing stream [Amos 5:24]." In the Epistle lesson, Paul refers to Christ's coming, when the dead will be raised first and then those who are alive "shall be caught up together with them in the clouds to meet the Sovereign in the air [1 Thess. 4:17]."

The Gospel is Jesus' parable of the wise and foolish maidens, told by Jesus to enlighten the disciples about the realm of heaven. The crux of the story is that "when the foolish took their lamps, they took no oil with them; but the wise took flasks of oil with their lamps [Matt. 25:3–4]." And when the delayed bridegroom came, it was only the wise women who got to go to the marriage feast. Tell this story to the children, using an oil lamp and a flask of oil.

Further illustrate the theme of being prepared by indicating that the realm of heaven is like going on a wilderness camping trip without a flashlight or a poncho (show the flashlight and the poncho). You've got to be prepared for the dark of night and the chance of rain. The passage concludes with Jesus' injunction: "Watch therefore, for you know neither the day nor the hour [Matt. 25:13]." Encourage the children to "be prepared."

Prayer: O God, help me to be wise. Help me to be prepared for your coming. Amen.

PENTECOST 26

Use Them or Lose Them!

Lesson 1:   Zephaniah 1:7, 12–18
Lesson 2:   1 Thessalonians 5:1–11
Gospel: Matthew 25:14–30

Theme: Talents
Resources: Fifteen silver dollars

Development: The Gospel is Jesus' parable of the talents, used to help the disciples understand the realm of heaven. People are entrusted with talent and expected to use it for the glory of God: "For to all who have will more be given, and they will have abundance; but from those who have not, even what they have will be taken away [Matt. 25:29]." Use them or lose them!

Tell this captivating story using fifteen silver dollars at the appropriate point in the story. You may want to invite some of the children to act out the parable, but in my experience, the acting often impedes the communication of the story rather than enabling it. Lots of eye contact will help the characters and their words come alive, especially "Well done, good and faithful servant; you have been faithful over a little, I will set you over much; enter into the joy of your Sovereign [Matt. 25:21]." Apply the parable to the children by assuring them that God has indeed given them talents and by inviting them to share what their talents are and how they're using them.

Affirm their talents with enthusiasm, and encourage them to use them this week for the glory of God. A simple word of encouragement from you can give them confidence and a vital sense of self-worth.

Prayer: Creator, may I use my talent for your glory. Amen.

PENTECOST 27

The Great Surprise

Lesson 1: Ezekiel 34:11–16, 20–24
Lesson 2: 1 Corinthians 15:20–28
Gospel: Matthew 25:31–46

Theme: Caring in God's name
Resource: "A glorious throne" (a regal-looking chair)

Development: This Sunday marks the end of the season of Pentecost and of the liturgical church year. Follow up the parable of the talents considered last week by telling Jesus' parable of the great judgment so that the children will be familiar with the content and rhythm of Jesus' teaching. You may recall this parable being presented effectively in *Godspell*, a musical based on the Gospel according to Matthew. The writer there caught the flavor of surprise and shock that is at the heart of the story.

Set the scene for the children: "When the Human One comes in glory, with all the angels, then that one will sit on a glorious throne. All the nations will be gathered before the Human One, who will separate them one from another as a shepherd separates the sheep from the goats, placing the sheep on the right, but the goats on the left [Matt. 25:31–33]." Sit, regally clothed if you wish, on a "glorious throne," a regal-looking chair, and for the purpose of the story, divide the children into two groups—"the sheep" and "the goats." Then tell the parable with lots of animation, especially when "the goats" ask: "O Sovereign, when did we see you hungry or thirsty or a stranger or naked or sick or in prison, and did not minister to you [Matt. 25:44]?" Close today by encouraging them to care in God's name, for by doing so they will have eternal life.

Prayer: Loving God, help me to care in your name. Amen.

INDEX OF SCRIPTURE READINGS
(Year A)

Micah

| 6:1–8 | Epiphany 4 |

Zephaniah

| 1:7, 12–18 | Pentecost 26 |

Matthew

1:18–25	Advent 4
2:1–12	Epiphany
2:13–15, 19–23	Christmas 1
3:1–12	Advent 2
3:13–17	Epiphany 1
4:1–11	Lent 1
4:12–23	Epiphany 3
5:1–12	Epiphany 4
5:13–16	Epiphany 5
5:17–26	Epiphany 6
5:27–37	Epiphany 7
5:38–48	Epiphany 8
6:1–6, 16–21	Ash Wednesday
7:21–29	Pentecost 2
9:9–13	Pentecost 3
9:35—10:8	Pentecost 4
10:24–33	Pentecost 5
10:34–42	Pentecost 6
11:2–11	Advent 3
11:25–30	Pentecost 7

Luke

2:1–20	Christmas Eve/Day
24:13–35	Easter 3

John

1:1–18	Christmas 2
1:29–41	Epiphany 2
3:1–17	Lent 2
4:5–42	Lent 3
9:1–41	Lent 4
10:1–10	Easter 4
11:17–45	Lent 5
13:1–17, 34	Maundy Thursday
14:1–14	Easter 5
14:15–21	Easter 6
17:1–11	Easter 7
18:1—19:42	Good Friday
20:1–18	Easter
20:19–23	Pentecost
20:19–31	Easter 2

Acts

1:1–14	Easter 7
2:1–21	Pentecost
2:14a, 22–32	Easter 2
2:14a, 36–47	Easter 3
6:1–9; 7:2a, 51–56	Easter 4

10:34–43	Epiphany 1 (Baptism)
10:34–48	Easter
17:1–15	Easter 5
17:22–31	Easter 6

Romans

1:1–7	Advent 4
3:21–28	Pentecost 2
4:1–9, 13–17	Lent 2
4:13–18	Pentecost 3
5:1–11	Lent 3
5:6–11	Pentecost 4
5:12–19	Pentecost 5
5:12–21	Lent 1
6:3–11	Pentecost 6
7:14–25a	Pentecost 7
8:6–19	Lent 5
8:9–17	Pentecost 8
8:18–25	Pentecost 9
8:26–30	Pentecost 10
8:31–39	Pentecost 11
9:1–5	Pentecost 12
11:13–16, 29–32	Pentecost 13
11:33–36	Pentecost 14
12:1–13	Pentecost 15
13:1–10	Pentecost 16
13:11–14	Advent 1

INDEX OF THEMES

Family	Advent 4, Christmas 1, Epiphany 3, Easter 2
Forgiveness	Epiphany 6, Pentecost 17
Friendship	Epiphany 7, Lent 2, Pentecost 7
Growth	Ash Wednesday, Lent 3, Pentecost 8, Pentecost 25
Guidance	Easter 3, Pentecost 23
Hearing	Pentecost 8
Hope	Easter, Pentecost 5, Pentecost 9
Humility	Maundy Thursday
Incarnation	Christmas, Christmas 2
Inheritance	Easter 2
Journey	Ash Wednesday, Lent 2
Joy	Lent 6
Justice	Epiphany 4
Last Supper	Maundy Thursday
Letters	Pentecost 21
Life	Easter 5
Light	Epiphany, Epiphany 1, Epiphany 5, Epiphany 9
Listening	Pentecost 13
Love	Epiphany 8, Pentecost 11, Pentecost 23
Messiah	Advent 2
Mission	Trinity Sunday, Pentecost 4, Pentecost 7
Music	Pentecost 5
Name	Advent 4
Obedience	Easter 4
Openness	Easter 4
Partnership	Pentecost 18
Passion	Lent 6
Passover	Epiphany 2